CALCULATED LIFE PLANNING
& GOAL SETTING

Bryan J. Gauthier

Calculated Life Planning And Goal Setting
Copyright © 2001 by Something Better Institute

Requests for information should be addressed to:
Something Better Institute
4022 E. Greenway Road
Suite 11-211
Phoenix, Arizona 85032-4760

Library of Congress Control Number: 2004093619

Gauthier, Bryan

Calculated Life Planning & Goal Setting/Bryan Gauthier

p.cm.

ISBN 0-9754852-0-2

Published In Phoenix, Arizona, by Something Better Institute

Printed in the United States of America.

Unless otherwise indicated, all scripture quotations are taken from *The King James* version of the Bible.

This Home Study Course provides the author's opinions and advice. It is not the intentions of the author (Bryan J. Gauthier) or the Publisher to render finalized legal, accounting or any other professional advice within this course.

In regards to the proper business licensing, legal procedures, accounting and tax matters, the author and publisher strongly suggest for the reader to seek additional advice of licensed professionals in the city, town, or community in which the reader may intend on starting a business enterprise.

The author and publisher disclaim any personal liability, loss, or risk incurred due to the usage or applications, directly or indirectly, or any information, procedures, or advice presented within this course.

This Book is dedicated to all the champions I feel God placed in my "Path" who influenced my life, by passing down their wisdom and insights to make my life and this course possible.

<u>Above all</u>, to the most giving mentor, My, Mother

<u>Pamela J. Gauthier.</u>

She reached her goals in life! And 8 days extra! 4/18/46-1/8/00 53 yrs.old
"She had a rare and dynamic drive to live for others! Full Page Dedication In Back Of Book

Set Life Goals

*Have you ever pondered what your end will show?
Have you ever feared your future and what it may hold?
Does your life sometimes feel empty-short of what it really
could be? Perhaps there's something inside that you need to
see? Look again into yourself. It's there your potential smiles
at hope. It's there you see personal conquest and pass through
boundaries when some say it can't be done. If you are willing
and you desire to discover your predestined path, if you know
you must find a way, then I'll tell you friend, yield this day.
Why not look back to your dreams and realize that all things
are possible if you only dare to believe? From this day
forward it's goals you will need to succeed! They'll give you a
purpose to rise afresh as the likeness of a child with energy to
seize a day of playing. It's God given goals from this day forth
that will renew your spirit and inspire you to complete your
course.*

*Sometimes a few more steps are all it takes to win. You've
crawled, you've walked, now it's time to run with clarity! Why
not begin to meditate upon your dreams and forget about the
fears? As you set aside doubts, you'll be able to stick out your
chin and withstand the punches of life. You'll stand firm with
momentum forward upon this incredible journey. Why not
achieve your goal with all your might? Don't look back, to the
left or to the right, because it's straight forward that you must
fight. Dream with hunger and desire, then reality will be
yours, and it is yours, and it is worth it! Life is a pattern time
and time again. It is filled with high achievers destined to win.
Now you know that you too, can be destined to be one, one to
win! Why not be the next champion to set the pace for those
who are wondering,
how they also can win?*

For your benefit,
Bryan J. Gauthier

HTTP://WWW.BETTERPATHS.COM

LIFE CHANGING CHALLENGE & TESTIMONY

Are you a candidate for the "Something Better" achievement award? *A 7 day Caribbean or Mexican Riviera Cruise.* Is your testimony one that would show the most improved before and after lifestyle changes?

Please send us your testimony and share with us what you personally got out of this study course and how it benefited you most. Knowing this study course helped you get on the right path, "your path," makes this study course complete.

Please mail your testimony & a filled out copy of the permission form below to:
Something Better Institute, 4022 E. Greenway Road, Suite 11-211, Phoenix, Arizona 85032-4760

PERMISSION FOR USE OF TESTIMONY

Attn: **Bryan J. Gauthier & Something Better Institute, you have my permission to use my testimony at Seminars, Radio, TV, and in any other forms of advertisements.**

Address:_____

City:_____**State**_____**Zip**_____

Email Address: _____

Phone #:_____

Alternate #: _____

Date:_____

Print Name

Signature

Table of Contents

Section 1

Personalized
Dream Sheets

Bryan Gauthier

Personalized Dream Sheet For

_____
(YOUR FULL NAME)

Answer the following questions as though you get
to have a fresh start for your life. Try to imagine
that you get to choose your new life from a menu
that has no limitations. Suppose that anything you
choose from your life menu is possible and will be
granted. How will you live? What will you be
content with having or being in every area of your
life? Make it as real as possible and dare to have
a big vision!

Please try to move along at a steady pace,
knowing that you can always make changes. If
anything, list key words or phrases so that you can
come back to any area at a later time to rewrite
your ideas more clearly.

Lifetime Contentment Levels

Q: What are some major things you can think of that you want out of life?

A:_____
_____
_____

Q: What are some of the main characteristics you desire in a mate?

A: _____
_____
_____

Q: What are some of the main characteristics you desire for your close friends to have?

A: _____
_____
_____

Q: Over the next five to ten years, if I could build my business or career as big as I wanted and I had the option to choose, what amount of spendable money would I be content with having per month for the rest of my life, no matter how big it gets? (Consider an amount of spendable money after all bills are paid.)

A: $_____ per month.

Next 2 - 5 Years Contentment Levels

Q: Would I be willing to take a few steps back with my current lifestyle & spending, knowing that in two to five years from now I could be at least three to five times further ahead financially & have more time off to enjoy my success?

A: Yes_____ No_____

Q: If all my bills were paid off, what would I do with the extra money?

A:_____

_____

_____

_____

Q: What If I could work doing anything I enjoyed and was able to choose the exact amount of pay for the day, what would I be content with earning per day?

A: $_____ per day.

Q: What if I could work doing anything I enjoyed and was able to choose the exact amount of pay for the week, what would I be content with earning per week?

A: $_____ per week.

Q: What if I could work doing anything I enjoyed and was able to choose the exact amount of pay for the month, what would I be content with earning per month, starting immediately?

A: $_____ per month.

Q: If I could justify working less hours in a day by earning more money during the hours I work in a day, while still reaching my daily contentment level, what would be the minimum amount of hours a day that I would want to work?

A: _____ hrs.

Q: If I could justify working less days in a week by earning more money during the days I work in a week while still reaching my weekly contentment level, what would be the minimum amount of days a week that I would want to work?

A: _____ days.

Q: Would I want to take any months off in a year?

A: _____. If yes, when and how often?

A: _____.

Q: Would I want to take any weeks off in a year?

A: _____. If yes, when and how often?

A: _____.

Q: If I could take a vacation anywhere or for any length of time, where would I go?

List any places that you know you would like to start vacationing each year, in order of interest.

A:_____

_____

_____

Q: What are some lifestyle things or activities I desire to do? (Example:) scuba diving, etc.

A:_____

_____

_____

Q: If I could choose my perfect home, approximately how many square feet would I want it to be in order to be content for the rest of my life? **A:** _____sq. ft. How many bedrooms would I want it to have? **A:** _____ bedrooms. How many bathrooms? **A:** _____ bathrooms.

How big of an office? **A:** _____sq. ft.

How big of a garage? **A:** _____ car garage.

How much land would I want my home on? **A:** _____

Are there any other things I would want included with my perfect home?

A:_____

_____

Q: If I could comfortably afford the vehicles of my choice for myself & family, what would they be?

A:_____

_____

Q: If I could have my choice of any toys for myself & family, what would they be?

A: (Example:) boat, etc.

_____

_____.

Q: If I could comfortably afford a second home or vacation home, where would I want it to be?

A:_____

_____

Q: If I had a lot of earned time off or free time, would I be interested in seriously thinking about remedies or ideas that will improve the lives of others? **A:** _____. If yes, on the next page list all ways you might be able to think of at the moment, weather fulfilled by you or others. Again, make it as real as possible and dare to have a big vision! (If anything, list keys words or phrases so that you can come back to this area at a later time in order to write your ideas more clearly.) Also keep in mind there are other people out there who you can partner with or they can help connect your ideas into a funneling system which is geared and committed to reach everybody by bringing everyone's ideas together in usable ways. "Remember, all are unique and have something different to offer others, the key is to recognize the needs around us that are obvious and fill them by using the information that is in us." (A lot of needed things are waiting for someone to step forward to start them.)

By answering all of the previous questions you have just made a huge step in the direction of eliminating fuzzy thinking. From now on your decisions will be influenced around the desires and contentment's you have just identified for your life. Now you will be able to make wiser considerations and choices with the opportunities that present themselves in your life. Mainly by knowing that you can give them your stamp of approval or disapproval based off of whether or not they conflict with your contentment levels in life.

Thoughts & Notes

"I CAN'T CHANGE" IS JUST A POOR EXCUSE FOR NOT
SUCCEEDING. I'M HERE TO TELL YOU, YES YOU CAN!
NOT ONLY CAN YOU CHANGE, YOU CAN HAVE GOOD
SUCCESS AND IT WILL BE WORTH IT!"

Section 2

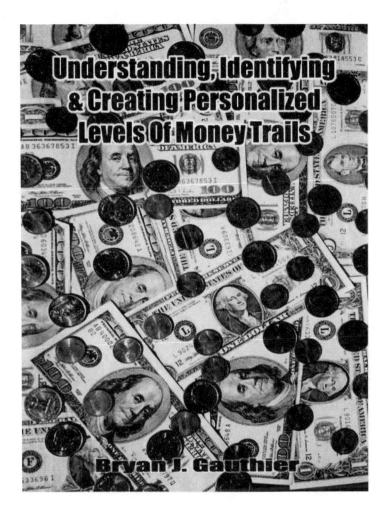

Understanding, Identifying & Creating Personalized Levels Of Money Trails

Bryan J. Gauthier

By

Bryan J. Gauthier

Money Trails

The next few pages have been created for the purpose of stimulating the way you think toward ideas, also how to see more of the big picture involved in what an idea is actually worth overall. Are all opportunities created equal? I don't think so, but I do believe certain opportunities can be placed under a specific category, which may be considered equal in the sense of exposing the opportunities overall value. The system I'm writing about is called money trails. To better explain, I am reminded of a friend and mentor of mine, Mick Casey from Fallon, Nevada. Some time ago he shared a valuable bit of information with me stating, that in most cases it is easier to make a lot of money than it is to make a little. He went on to say that making smaller amounts often leave less room for mistakes than larger amounts. At our beginning stages one wrong or careless move can wipe out our resources. One person may be spending 8 hours of their time picking up 1 dollar bills each day on one trail while using up a lot more energy than another person who is spending 5 hours of there time picking up 100 dollar bills or thousand dollar bills on another trail. The point is that there are different trails available for all of us. We would all like to start on bigger trails and some may, but for most of us we have used the smaller trails to purchase the means of getting bigger trails. Today Mick Casey is involved with large amounts of real estate, giving programs and other endeavors, but he didn't start out that way. As a 10-year-old boy he had 10 cows that he raised on his father's ranch. At the age of 15 he continued to use his profits from raising and selling cows to buy more cows until after high school he had over 150 that where paid for. At that time 10 cows could pay for a brand new pickup truck. Instead of spending his profits, he purchased a 40-acre ranch at the age of 18, the next year another 40-acre ranch. From there he continued to invest his money in buying land, sub dividing, selling, and other endeavors. (For Example:) He purchased one piece of land for $11,000 and sold it in three years for $56,000.

A-Penny Trail

A-Quarter Trail

A-Dollar Trail

A-Hundred Dollar Trail

A-Thousand Dollar Trail

Q: What money trail or trails would be best for me to start with, based off my current amount of knowledge or resources available?

A: _____

Q: What lengths of time would I need to commit of myself on each trail in order to earn enough money for purchasing a higher producing money trail?

A: _____

Example & Effects from Working Within the Following Trails

A-Penny Trail

A Penny Trail: If you worked 8 hours a day, you would have to pick up 10,000 pennies to earn $100.00. Effects: Possibly bruises & cuts, band aids on the fingers, also the burden of carrying 10,000 pennies in a sack may eventually cause back problems or burn out on life if done for to many years. Often times it takes almost all of your thinking and concentration to pick up 10,000 pennies within 8 hours. Penny trails may also result in less time and less energy to see beyond the end of a day. Less time & energy can have the likeness of a mountain which blocks a beautiful sunset or a better money trail. The sunset, or money trail is definitely there, but usually not seen unless we can rise above the mountain to see it. Of course with creativity, we can always find an easier and faster way to get the same job done with less effort and more efficiency. (I would consider using a super powered shop vacuum!)

Q: If you were to consider one of your ideas that may match this trail, about how much might you earn or save in 2 years or 5 years?

A: 2 years $_____ 5 years $_____

Q: What options can you think of doing to match the income of a Penny Trail?

A:_____

_____

_____

Now narrow your choices down to only three. They can be skill or knowledge related or simply preference.

Options: 1._____, 2._____, 3._____.

A-Quarter Trail

A Quarter Trail: If you worked 7 hours a day, you would have to pick up 1,000 quarters to earn $250.00. Effects: More time to think and time to look off to the horizon to see bigger money trails, or other opportunities that may be relative to your mission in life. Instead of picking up money every step, you may be able to pick up a quarter say once every twenty steps or so. Leaving you twenty steps to look around to possibly spot a waterfall nearby flowing with dollar bill opportunities.

Q: If you were to consider one of your ideas that may match this trail, about how much might you earn or save in 2 years or 5 years?

A: 2 years $_____ 5 years $_____

Q: What options can you think of doing to match the income of a Quarter Trail?

A:_____
_____
_____

Now narrow your choices down to only three. They can be skill or knowledge related or simply preference.

Options: 1._____, 2._____, 3._____.

A-Dollar Trail

A Dollar Trail: If you worked 6 hours a day, you would have to pick up 750 dollar bills to earn $750.00. Effects: A lot more time to look around for bigger money trails, and the ability to save in cash reserves such as having at least $10,000 in savings at all times. On this trail you can start dreaming with more enthusiasm, knowing that the financial reserves in your savings account not only represent the ability to consider bigger money trails, but also the realistic abilities to set them in motion, immediately.

Q: If you were to consider one of your ideas that may match this trail, about how much might you earn or save in 2 years or 5 years?

A: 2 years $_____ 5 years $_____.

Q: What options can you think of doing to match the income of a Dollar Trail?

A:_____
_____
_____

Now narrow your choices down to only three. They can be skill or knowledge related or simply preference.

Options: 1._____, 2._____, 3._____.

A-Hundred Dollar Trail

A: 100 Dollar Trail: If you worked 5 hours a day, you would have to pick up 20 one hundred dollar bills to earn $2,000.00. Effects: A lot of freedom and a lot of choices. On this trail you may have access to some serious cash resources to relate new dreams to and plenty of cash to hire and pay key personnel for managing the areas you need not be involved in. On this trail you can free up more time for doing your most valuable functions. Dreaming, planning, protecting, strategizing and seeing that new ideas are put in effect. At this point, you must clearly know what it takes to keep you performing at your best. I perform best when I can run as hard as possible, stopping momentarily only at the borderlines which I know I need a time of refreshing and rejuvenation. I get rejuvenated through vacations and dream building breaks. (Some of my best ideas have come to me while watching the ocean, and sitting in the sand at some tropical beach!)

Q: If you were to consider one of your ideas that may match this trail, about how much might you earn or save in 2 years or 5 years?

A: 2 years $_____ 5 years $_____ .

Q: What options can you think of doing to match the income of a 100 Dollar Trail?

A:_____
_____
_____ .

Now narrow your choices down to only three. They can be skill or knowledge or simply preference.

Options: 1._____, 2._____, 3._____ .

A-Thousand Dollar Trail

A: 1,000 Dollar Trail: If you worked 4 hours a day, you would have to pick up at least 2.5, thousand dollar bills to earn $2,500.00 or more. Effects: More freedom and a lot of choices. On this trail, it's up to you how far you want to go in relation to reaching your destiny.   Quantum leaps toward changing the world for the good are definitely within your grasp.   At this level you can transform your efforts from duplication to major levels of multiplication. Remember your contentment levels, at this point you will definitely be able to live within them, and also have the options to use them. At this point you have the option of channeling all your overflows into ways to help benefit others and yourself, by being able to live vicariously through them as their lives become transformed through your giving programs.

Q: If you were to consider one of your ideas that may match this trail, about how much might you earn or save in 2 years or 5 years?

A: 2 years $_____ 5 years $_____ .

Q: What options can you think of doing to match the income of a 1,000 Dollar Trail?

A:_____
_____
_____ .

Now narrow your choices down to only three. They can be skill or knowledge related or simply preference.

Options: 1._____, 2._____, 3._____ .

Now transfer your top three choices from each trail to as follows:

Top Three Options For Each Money Trail

A Penny Trail:

1._____, 2._____, 3._____.

A Quarter Trail:

1._____, 2._____, 3._____.

A Dollar Trail:

1._____, 2._____, 3._____.

A 100 Dollar Trail:

1._____, 2._____, 3._____.

A 1,000 Dollar Trail:

1._____, 2._____, 3._____.

My life Overview/Calculated Planning

Q: How old am I right now? **A:** ____years old.

Q: How old, at the least would I like to live to be?
A: ____years old.

Q: Which money trail could I see myself starting at first?
A: _____Trail.

Q: How old will I be upon getting started?

A: ____years old.

Q: How many years at the most do I think it will take to advance to a higher money trail? **A:** ____years. **Q:** What money trail option would I consider starting at that point?

A: _____ **Q:** About how old will I be upon starting?

A: ____years old.

Q: How many years at the most do I think it will take to advance to a higher money trail? **A:** ____years. **Q:** What money trail option would I consider starting at that point?

A: _____ **Q:** About how old will I be upon starting?

A: ____years old.

Q: How many years at the most do I think it will take to advance to a higher money trail? **A:** ____years. **Q:** What money trail option would I consider starting at that point?

A: _____

Q: About how old will I be upon starting? **A:** ____years old.

Q: How many years at the most do I think it will take to advance to a higher money trail? **A:** ____years. **Q:** What money trail option would I consider starting at that point?

A: _____

Q: About how old will I be upon starting? **A:** ____years old.

That's great!

I'll bet you didn't realize setting goals and making plans could become so easy. Keep in mind, none of these example money trails are set in stone, the whole purpose is to help stimulate your thinking and create a way you can relate opportunities to a value system. If needed, you may customize or alter them to better fit your own ideas or needs. The more information and ideas, that you can get documented, the better. As you move on you will always be able to come back and adjust the details and do the polishing up when needed.

Right now it's time to develop some strategies to help you move from one money trail to the next. There are several possible ways of doing this. All it takes is some thought and planning. First you must begin by changing how you think of the future against how you see yourself in the future. Here are some sample strategies you can apply to almost any plan or goal regarding choices, careers, business, or investments.

A. Set some short term goals: 3 month, 6 month, 9 month, or 1 year. Goals should be very specific. Goals can be money oriented, as in a savings plan (no savings plan is too small, remember: you've got to start somewhere). Goals can be time oriented, as in taking time to research how to invest your money and time to learn something new. Goals can be knowledge oriented as in learning more information, meeting new people who can help you, or learning a new skill.

B. Stretch your mind to see new possibilities. Make it a habit to read books, listen to tapes, or watch videos that may help motivate and clarify your thinking. Try to spend at least 2 to 5 hours a week toward building your dreams. Have sessions in which you can evaluate your plans, goals and strategies of becoming more effective or efficient. Use your God given imagination to create something from nothing. The bible says you are made in the image and likeness of God. Knowing this, you can be assured that the ability of creative thinking is definitely in you. In most cases it just has to be developed and strengthened, therefore start by allowing your imagination to soar above and beyond what may be considered the normal ways of thinking.

C. Read biographies of what other people have done in their lives, learn from their strengths, and learn from their weaknesses. Don't try to invent something that someone else has already perfected. There's lots of information available to learn from others successes. Their stories are in biography books, the Internet, government web sites, newspapers, magazines, or journals on business and finance. So read a little, and then read a lot. Make it a habit to plan your reading and research time.

D. If the information provided is effective, consider taking some classes at a local community college or vocational training school. There are also many free training programs sponsored by city and county governments and many church organizations. There are many classes available on business, job skills, finance, computers, etc. This will not only stimulate your learning abilities but also open your mind and open new doors to meet new people who may be able to help you reach your goals. Any training you consider should always be relative toward reaching your goals or mission in life. Knowing this, you will save a lot of time by not getting misguided or sidetracked to an area that has nothing to do with what you need to be learning.

E. Make it a habit to keep your life in perspective and under control. Try not to neglect the basics in life, such as being thankful for what you have or don't have. Each day I have made it a point to be thankful for the simplicities of life. Upon opening my eyes each morning I thank God for a healthy mind and a healthy body. I thank God for another day to be alive and the ability to be productive. I'm thankful that he's got my life under control, even when the challenges may logically say different some times. I'm thankful for my family & friends, I'm thankful for the future he has prepared for me, I'm thankful for the spirit of happiness, I'm thankful for the finances he has provided, and I'm thankful for the people God has placed within my sphere of influence. This may sound a little simple minded, but I've seen how incredibly powerful an attitude of thanksgiving can be. I believe God responds to us in the same way a parent would respond to a child that is incredibly thankful for anything that their parent may have given them. Verses another child who no matter what you give them, always complains or gripes about what you didn't give. Honestly, which child would you give more too? Regardless, the bible clearly states that the way to effectively enter into his presence is through thanks giving, not give me, give me, give me. Once we can learn to be thankful for anything he has given us, we can then be in the proper place to ask for more, so that what we are given will produce results in our lives that will be pleasing to God and mankind. (Try it! Just say thank you for anything and then try to make it a habit that is consistent in your life.)

Which Gems Do I Pick Up?

You may know this already, or perhaps you will soon discover the interesting fact about opportunities. As you speak with a lot of seasoned entrepreneurs, you will hear more and more about hundreds of opportunities that are all around us everyday. You will soon discover yourself that there are literally hundreds of avenues to choose from in relation to your own personality and desires. So at this point, we go back to that precious word, wisdom. With good leadership and wise delegation, it is very possible to achieve large amounts of goals and dreams. But somewhere in there comes a fine line where you must ask yourself, "How can I narrow the choices down to just the ones really worth choosing?" Remember this, you can always make more money but you cannot make more time. On the other hand more money will free up time. That is, if you create your structures to do that. To bring out my point, let's look at life and what it really is again. Average life on earth = 70 years or 25,567.5 days. Your goal on earth = to reach your full God given potential. Reaching your full potential involves a lifetime commitment of choosing the best choice from amongst all the other choices. So how do we know how to choose the best choice from amongst many, perhaps even hundreds? The answer is this: by putting a measurable value which is understandable on each option or choice. (We have provided example diagrams on the next few pages.)

Looking at phase A, let's use the profession construction for an example. Say you have skills in being a landscaper, a plumber, and a concrete finisher. Is it going to be more profitable for you to try and combine them together into one business or choose one and become very efficient at just one? If you decide to choose just one, then you can choose the best by placing three measurable values on each one. In phase A, with 1 crew on an 8-hour day, you might make $500 dollars a day profit in all three choices. Perhaps one makes less than the others and that might be a reason to cancel it out after considering the other two values. If you are considering going into a business that already exists and you're not sure what they make in a day, then just simply start asking business owners what they make in a day. Not only that, most business owners are more than happy to answer your questions to help you get your own thing going. Simply asking questions can become one of your greatest tools for success.

"PHASE A"

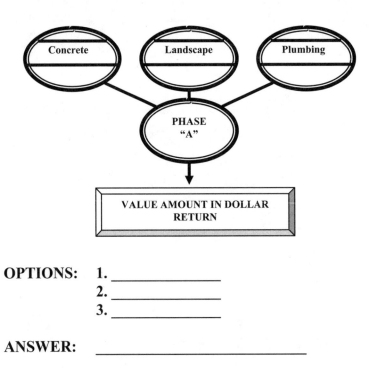

OPTIONS: 1. _____
          2. _____
          3. _____

ANSWER: _____

Looking at phase B: Using a scale of 1-10, decide which one you enjoy the most. Which one will give the most satisfaction over the short and long haul? Which one would have the highest potential for growth while still enjoying it the most?

PHASE B:

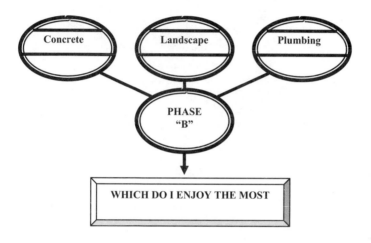

OPTIONS: 1. _____
           2. _____
           3. _____

ANSWER: _____

Now consider phase C. Using the diagram with a scale of 1-10, decide which one will give you more free time to enjoy your rewards and time to think and prepare for the next phase of accomplishment in your life goals program. This should also be in relation to your contentment level toward dollar returns, and your enjoyment of the venture.

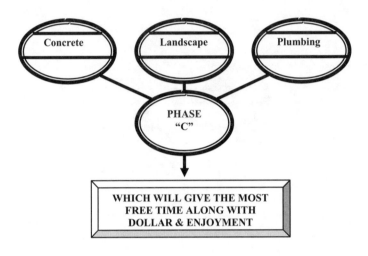

OPTIONS: 1. _____
          2. _____
          3. _____

ANSWER: _____

Last of all, consider phase D.

This one changed my thinking early on in life. As a new and untamed entrepreneur, my imagination developed lots of ways to make money from ideas. Today is similar to then and today there are even more ways to effect the world or make money. Looking at life for what it really is and knowing what the mentality of mankind is as a whole globally, you will discover lots of ways to capitalize on the needs and desires of mankind. Looking from this perspective, you can clearly see that there are a lot of corrupt markets in which to make money. We've all been created with a free will, a freedom of choice to do as we please. Personally, knowing what I know now, I believe wholeheartedly that we all have been born with qualifications to single handedly effect the world in our lifetime. Knowing this, I will ask you the same thing that was impressed upon my heart early on. This question canceled out a lot of my ideas once I pondered them thoroughly and answered them honestly. With every idea and concept you consider, ask yourself, what good is in it? How will it affect people around me and the world as a whole? Don't be afraid to answer this honestly, or feel that you may jeopardize not having enough ideas. Again, as you climb, you will find so many legitimate opportunities that you can't get to them all in a lifetime. I personally believe that we are all born with good hearts and good intentions to help others. But to stay true to those qualities and strengths throughout a lifetime involves consistent integrity and choices that really are not that hard. It can be done with obedience, wisdom, and the simple ability to choose a path that is honorable to God, fellow man and woman, and the benefit of this whole earth overall. Yet sad but true, a lot of people do choose to take the same effort it takes to choose honest, meaningful paths and move without conviction, full speed ahead into ventures that corrupt not only their targeted prospects, but the world in general. I'm emphasizing this because I know life goes by fast and it requires quick decisions at times. With quick decisions, we must spend quality time concentrating and thinking of what we are doing.

We personally are the ones driving our vehicle through life and we need to stop at times and realize that we are responsible for the passengers and pedestrians. I'm reminded of a quote stated by the philosopher, Rolamay. He spoke on the Cowardus of Conformity. "So often we can look around at what other people are doing and we can conform." I've seen this temperament time and time again in the world of free enterprise. It's easy to say, 'Well, there are so many other people pumping garbage into the world, is it really going to make any difference if I do, too?' Truth and Wisdom say, "Yes! It Will!"

What Good Is In It?

For Me:

_____
_____
_____
_____
_____

For Those Around Me:

_____
_____
_____
_____
_____

For The World As A Whole:

_____
_____
_____
_____
_____

IT'S BEEN PROVEN THROUGHOUT HISTORY, TIME & TIME AGAIN, THAT ONE MAN OR WOMAN CAN SINGLE HANDEDLY, THROUGH LIFE GOALS, EFFECT THE WORLD.
(FOR THE GOOD!)

Know Your Stuff

Knowledge brings confidence. You have learned some basic principles in clarifying your goals, sub goals, and life goal. With defining your goals, you now know what to do your homework on. Whatever the field of endeavor you are aiming at, know your stuff. Learn as much as possible relative to your goals. Develop a habit to read books, listen to tapes, or watch videos that give information pertaining to your goals. Use your study time wisely and don't waste time reading information that is not relative to your goals, in the most part. Perhaps your interest is to do art work, maybe even to be the most advanced or on the cutting edge of the market. If so, learn as much as possible and then consider new concepts never done and learn about things to make it possible. Once you're sure of your directions in life, all you have to do is look for the key information relative to that direction. Again, don't waste time reading information that has nothing to do with the direction you're heading toward, in the most part.

Study The Markets Of Your Venture

Know the facts of the market. Ask yourself questions such as these in order to help you begin to understand the facts of a market and how it relates to your business. Number one - "What months might be slow in sales compared to others?" Number two - "What can I do to compensate for the slower months?" Number three - "What months might have double the amounts of sales?" And Number four - "If so, will I be able to handle the work load?" Be informed. The informed entrepreneur knows ahead of time about potential problems or possible situations. Do your homework and you will always end up on top and on the cutting edge of your ventures.

How To Read Five Books
In The Same Time It Takes To Read One

This can be done by highlighting or underlining just the key information relative to your goals. As you practice doing this with every book you read, it will then be possible to reread and browse through five books in the same time it takes to read one. Keep in mind that the mind is like a tire with a slow leak. The mind needs to be constantly renewed. So while you are relaxing, you can consume five books by just reading key points.

How To Choose A Business/Organization Name

The purpose of the business or organization consists of what?

A:_____

_____

_____

_____

Now think of a short creative title to sum it all up. If your business deals with only one type of service or product, you might consider using your name with the description of the service or product. An example would be this: Rob Smith Remodeling or Cheryl's Housecleaning. If you intend to have a wide variety of products or services, you might be wise to sum it all up under one heading such as: Rob Smith Company, then write the descriptions of products or services under that name. I suggest you use a name that products and services can be added to. The reason is that if you do expand, you will save time and money by not having to change your checks, bank account, stationary, business cards, etc. Knowing this, you may choose to create a name without your own name in it. Perhaps you're interested in shipping products overseas or receiving products from overseas. A good example to describe a wide range business like this might be something like Global Traders or World Products, etc. Then again you might wish to use your own name followed by a word that has a wide description such as Smith's Global Trading or Smith's World Products. It's up to you which method to use, preferably the one that excites you the most!

Thoughts & Notes

Create a name for a product or service using the chart below.

Example 1: A food warming bowl with a built in heating system operated by batteries. Think of five ways to describe the example product using the headings below.

DESCRIPTION	IT DOES WHAT?	BENEFITS
1. Bowl with heating plate on the bottom.	Heats your food instantly.	Excellent For Traveling or to use at work.
2.		
3.		
4.		
5.		

Now compile the information into the most appropriate business or product names to describe the example business of selling portable warming bowls.

Choices: 1:_____

2:_____

3:_____

Choosing the right name of a product or service is very important in marketing it effectively. Now use the same method as above with your own product or service

Product or Service:_____

DESCRIPTION	IT DOES WHAT?	BENEFITS
1.		
2.		
3.		
4.		
5.		

Again, compile the information into the most appropriate business or product name.

Choices: 1:_____
2:_____
3:_____

For additional study pertaining to all aspects of business... read our study course: *"Becoming An Entrepreneur"*
"A PERSONAL STEP-BY-STEP GUIDE TO DISCOVERING, BEGINNING & SUCCESSFULLY DEVELOPING A PROFITABLE BUSINESS"

To purchase this book, visit our website below

THOUGHTS & NOTES

Thoughts & Notes

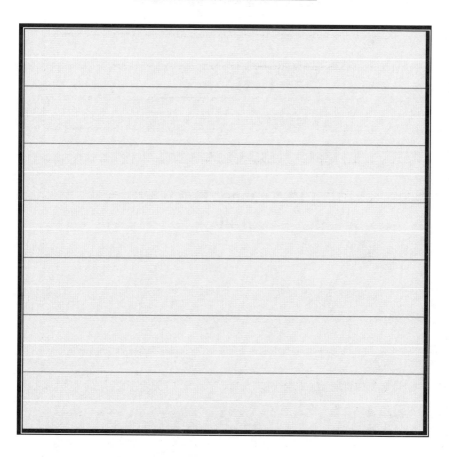

Task Needing Completion In Order of Importance

1.	11.
2.	12.
3.	13.
4.	14.
5.	15.
6.	16.
7.	17.
8.	18.
9.	19.
10.	20.

Section 3

110%
High Achiever
Thinking & Insights

110 Success Keys
Total

By

Bryan J. Gauthier

110%
High Achiever
Thinking & Insights

110 success keys total

IF YOU
FALL DOWN
GET UP!

Rollerblading
not recommended!

Bryan J. Gauthier

Preparing For The Battle

GOOD SUCCESS CAN ONLY BE ASSURED WHEN WE LEARN TO USE OUR TOOLS. WORDS IN THE FORM OF QUOTES, INSIGHTS AND PRINCIPLES ARE THE TOOLS WE NEED TO ACHIEVE **GOOD SUCCESS**. IF WE HAVE THEM MEMORIZED WE WILL THEN BE ABLE TO ACT UPON THEM AT ANY GIVEN MOMENT THAT A SITUATION MAY PRESENT ITSELF OR REQUIRE A DECISION TO TAKE ACTION. KNOWING ACCURATE PRINCIPLES AHEAD OF TIME EQUIPS US WITH THE ABILITY TO MAKE THE RIGHT CHOICES AND AT THE RIGHT TIMES. "IF TODAY YOU ARE WILLING TO DO WHAT MOST WON'T, SOMEDAY SOON YOU'LL SEE WHAT MOST CAN'T."

1. **<u>CHANGE IS KEY:</u>** IF YOU CONTINUE TO DO THE SAME THINGS AND EXPECT BETTER RESULTS, USUALLY IT WILL NEVER HAPPEN. OFTEN TIMES BEFORE WE CAN MOVE FORWARD WITH SUCCESS HABITS, WE MUST FIRST UNLEARN OUR FAILURE HABITS. I'VE FOUND THAT THE ONLY EFFECTIVE WAY TO TRULY BREAK A HABIT IS TO REPLACE IT WITH A BETTER HABIT. (EXAMPLE: REPLACE SMOKING WITH A JOGGING PROGRAM, ETC.)

2. **<u>DETERMINED IS KEY:</u>** WITH ENOUGH COMMIT-MENT, YOU REALLY CAN CREATE YOUR LIFE TO MATCH WHAT YOU WANT.

3. LIFE INVOLVES TIME FRAMES, THEREFORE THERE ARE CRUCIAL TIMES IN WHICH OPPORTUN-NITIES MAY PRESENT THEMSELVES AND WE NEED TO KNOW WHEN TO SPEED UP OUR ACTIONS SO WE DON'T MISS OUT OR FALL BEHIND IN OUR RACE TOWARD OUR POTENTIAL.

4. **<u>RENEWAL IS KEY:</u>** ALWAYS KNOW WHAT IT TAKES TO KEEP YOU PERFORMING AT YOUR BEST. RUN AS HARD AS YOU CAN AND SCHEDULE JUST ENOUGH VACATIONS OR BREAKS THAT YOU MAY NEED IN ORDER TO STAY FRESH WITH VISION, CLARITY, AND ENERGY. ALSO BEWARE OF FATIGUE, IF IT DOES TAKE HOLD OF YOU, THAT'S WHEN YOUR BELIEF IN YOURSELF MAY TRY TO WALK OUT.

5. I HAVE FOUND THAT WE CAN USUALLY GET PAID AS MUCH AS WE ARE WILLING TO GET ORGANIZED IN! (ORGANIZATION IS A KEY TO THE DUPLICATION OF OUR TIME, EFFORTS, AND PROFITS.)

6. **TEMPORARY SACRIFICES:** IF TODAY YOU ARE WILLING TO DO WHAT MOST WON'T, SOMEDAY SOON YOU'LL SEE WHAT MOST CAN'T.

7. **ANSWERS FOLLOW FAITH:** I CAN LOOK BACK AT WHERE I STARTED AND I REALIZE I HAD NO PERFECTED SYSTEMS, BUT I DID HAVE BIG DREAMS. THE DREAM ITSELF HAS TAUGHT ME WHAT TO DO AND PROVIDED THE ENERGY NEEDED TO PRESS FORWARD TOWARD WHERE TO GO IN ORDER TO LEARN HOW TO DO IT.

8. **TODAYS STRUGGLES PROVIDE LESSONS FOR LONG TERM SUCCESS:** BY BUILDING SOMETHING FROM THE GROUND UP YOU WILL REMEMBER ALL THE BEST PRINCIPLES INVOLVED IN KEEPING IT RUNNING AT ITS BEST.

9. **ATTENTION SINGLES:** CHOOSE YOUR MATE WISELY, BECAUSE THE PERSON THAT YOU MARRY CAN HAVE A HUGE IMPACT ON YOUR LIFE. THE RIGHT OR WRONG PERSON CAN BE ONE OF THE FOLLOWING: THE MAJORITY OF YOUR HAPPINESS OR THE MAJORITY OF YOUR UNHAPPINESS.

10. **UNDERSTAND THIS:** *IT IS WORTH IT! IT IS BEYOND WORTH IT!* STRUGGLES & FAILURES ARE NO REASON TO QUIT AND ARE OFTEN JUST PART OF THE EDUCATION PROCESS REQUIREMENTS NEEDED BEFORE YOU BECOME FULLY EQUIPPED TO REACH YOUR PURPOSE IN LIFE.

11. **DECIDE** TODAY THAT YOU WILL NEVER EVER QUIT AND YOU **WILL** EVENTUALLY FIND THE MEANS TO GET WHERE YOU WANT TO GO.

12. **IN THE MULTITUDE OF COUNSELORS THERE IS SAFETY:** WHEN MAKING ANY BIG DECISIONS, IT'S CRITICAL TO DISCUSS IT WITH YOUR CAREFULLY CHOSEN, WISE COUNSELORS – YOUR MENTORS.

13. **LIFE HAS SEASONS:** ONE SURE PATTERN OF LIFE IS UPS AND DOWNS FOR ALL OF US. AND I CAN TRULY TESTIFY THIS; IT WILL AND DOES EVENTUALLY CHANGE AND **WE CAN** LOOK BACK WITH EXTREME THANKFULNESS FOR HOW GREAT LIFE HAS BECOME BEING ON THE OTHER SIDE OF THE STORMS. ("KEEP YOUR FACE TO THE SUNSHINE & YOU CANNOT SEE THE SHADOWS"- HELLEN KELLER)

14. REGARDLESS OF WHAT PATHS YOU'RE ON IN LIFE, YOU'RE GOING TO FACE CHALLENGES. WHY NOT FACE THE ONES THAT LEAD YOU TOWARD *GOOD SUCCESS*?

15. BIG THOUGHTS AND BELIEF IN BIG THOUGHTS, CAN BE WHAT GIVES YOU THE ENERGY TO STEP OUT OF YOUR "TODAYS" SELF AND INTO "TOMORROWS" NEW SELF, DAY AFTER DAY, WITHOUT FATIGUE.

16. WHEN YOU THINK LARGER THAN OTHER PEOPLE THINK, YOU WILL FIND LARGER AMOUNTS OF ENERGY TO DO MORE THAN OTHER PEOPLE FEEL LIKE DOING.

17. IF YOUR DREAM IS BIG ENOUGH, THE IMPOSSIBILITIES WON'T COUNT. IMPOSSIBILITIES JUST MEAN THEY HAVEN'T BEEN FIGURED OUT.

18. <u>KEEPING MOMENTUM IS KEY:</u>
YOUR MOMENTUM PACE AFFECTS THE DIFFICULTY
OF YOUR CLIMB. CLIMB CAREFUL BUT FAST, SO
THAT THE DIFFICULTY IS HIDDEN BY THE CONCEN-
TRATION AND THRILL OF IT. CONVERSELY, CLIMB
CLUMSY BUT SLOW, AND YOU WILL BE AWARE OF
EVERY STEP. YOU WILL STUMBLE THINKING ONLY
OF HOW FAR YOU HAVE TO GO. (CONSIDER THE
POSSIBILITIES! WHAT IF YOU REALLY WENT ALL
OUT FOR 2 TO 5 YEARS? WHERE COULD YOU BE?)

19. <u>VISION IS KEY:</u> FIRST CHOOSE A DESTINATION.
SECOND, LOOK AT IT DAILY AND MEMORIZE ITS
APPEARANCE, THEN PURPOSE IN YOUR HEART TO
SEEING IT GO FROM THOUGHT TO BROUGHT IN
ACTIONS AND IT WILL HAPPEN.

20. <u>TUNEUPS ARE NOT JUST FOR CARS:</u>
UNDERSTAND THAT THROUGH LIFE YOU HAVE TO
CONSTANTLY REFOCUS YOURSELF IN THE
DIRECTION YOU WANT TO GO. BEWARE OF
BECOMING SIDETRACKED.

21. <u>START WHERE YOU'RE AT:</u> WHY NOT USE
THE SKILLS YOU HAVE NOW TO BUILD THE BRIDGE
TO WHAT YOU REALLY ENJOY DOING?

22. <u>DOUBT MAY TRY KNOCKING AT YOUR
DOOR:</u> IT'S HUMAN TO DOUBT DURING DIS-
COURAGING TIMES AND THAT'S OK, <u>**AS LONG AS**</u>
YOU ALWAYS ACT ON YOUR BELIEFS FROM THE
TIMES WHEN YOU WHERE NOT DISCOURAGED.

23. GOD HAS GIVEN US THE ABILITIES TO ACHIEVE OUR PURPOSE OR MAKE OUR BUSINESS WORK, BUT WE STILL HAVE TO FIGHT & DO WHAT HAS TO BE DONE IN ORDER TO MAKE SURE IT HAPPENS.

24. **CHANGE IS CONSTANT:** AS SOON AS WE ARE THROUGH CHANGING OUR LIFE, WE ARE THROUGH.

25. **DON'T SWEAT PETTY CRITICISM:** "IF CRITICISM HAD ANY REAL POWER, THE SKUNK WOULD HAVE BEEN EXTINCT YEARS AGO."
— *MARK TWAIN*

26. **TALKS CHEAP:** DON'T EVER THINK YOU CAN JUST BUILD A REPUTATION ON WHAT YOU'RE GOING TO DO. RATHER, BUILD YOUR REPUTATION ON WHAT YOU ARE DOING.

27. **GOD IS NOT PARTIAL:** ANYONE CAN ACHIEVE FINANCIAL SUCCESS. IF YOU KEEP ASKING GOD, HE WILL GIVE IT TO YOU WITH ONE CONDITION: ALLOW HIM TO TURN YOUR LIFE INSIDE OUT SO THAT HE CAN TRUST YOU WITH *GOOD* FINANCIAL *SUCCESS*. THEN YOU CAN USE YOUR SUCCESS FOR A PURPOSE ALONG WITH ENJOYING YOUR LIFE, AND NOT JUST VANITY.

28. DARE TO DO THE THINGS THAT OTHERS ONLY DARE TO DREAM.

29. ALL THINGS WORTH WHILE ARE DIFFICULT BEFORE THEY BECOME EASY.

30. **POSSIBLE IS A CHOICE:** I'VE OBSERVED THAT THE MAIN DIFFERENCE BETWEEN WHAT WE THINK IS POSSIBLE AND WHAT WE THINK IS IMPOSSIBLE IS OUR MIND SET. ALTHOUGH IT MAY NOT ALWAYS BE EASY, I TRULY DO BELIEVE THAT THERE IS ALWAYS A SOLUTION AND IT JUST NEEDS TO BE DISCOVERED & APPLIED.

31. **YOUR STEPPING OUT AND THAT'S GOOD:** SEEKING SUCCESS PROVES THAT YOU HAVE A WILLINGNESS TO ENDURE TEMPORARY DIS-COMFORT. BUT WHEN YOU COMPARE THE PAIN TO THE RESULTS, IT'S WORTH IT. I BELIEVE YOU'D DO IT OVER AND OVER AGAIN WITH MORE INTENSITY IF YOU COULD.

32. **FOLLOW THE FORMULA:** GOD CREATED US TO HAVE DOMINION OVER OUR LIVES. THIS PROCESS INVOLVES THOUGHTS, WISDOM, PRAYER, DECISIONS, AND APPLICATIONS.

33. **YOU ARE WHAT YOU EAT:** DEVELOP YOUR APPETITE TO SEEK WISDOM. WISDOM IS THE ESSENCE OF SEEING EVERYTHING AS IT REALLY IS. IN OUR DECISIONS, TRUE WISDOM EXPOSES ALL THE POSSIBILITIES WITHIN A SITUATION TO HELP US DISCERN THE BEST OUTCOME. — (*PONDER THE PATH OF THY FEET, AND LET ALL THY WAYS BE ESTABLISHED.* -PROVERBS 4:26.)

34. **BE CAREFUL OF WHERE YOUR TIME IS SPENT:** BE CAREFUL THAT YOU DON'T CONFUSE AN ACTIVITY WITH OBJECTIVITY.

35. THE RIGHT MINDSET MAKES ALL THE DIFFERENCE IN THE WORLD: DEVELOP A "NO EXCUSE" MENTALITY. AT THAT LEVEL IT DOESN'T MATTER WHAT YOUR CIRCUMSTANCES ARE. IT MAY NOT BE EASY BUT YOU WILL THEN KNOW THAT OUTSMARTING YOUR CIRCUMSTANCES IS A MUST IN ORDER TO WIN.

36. WE MAKE PROGRESS WHEN WE FOCUS ON OUR OWN ISSUES: SPEND MORE TIME THINKING ABOUT IMPROVING YOURSELF SO THAT YOU WON'T HAVE TIME TO THINK ABOUT CRITICIZING OR JUDGING OTHERS.

37. THIS IS THE DAY THAT COUNTS: WE DO NOT HAVE THE POWER TO GET BACK YESTERDAY. BUT WE DO HAVE THE POWER TO FULFILL TOMORROWS YESTERDAY. HAVE MASTERY OVER PROCRASTI-NATION, DO IT NOW!

38. DOCUMENTATION IS ONE OF THE TOP THREE KEYS TO SUCCESS: YOU CAN CONSTRUCT ANYTHING YOU CREATE IN YOUR MIND AS LONG AS YOU PUT THOSE THOUGHTS ON PAPER. A DREAM IN YOUR MIND THEN BECOMES WRITTEN REFER-ENCE MATERIAL. IT CAN THEN BE MEASURED, ALTERED, AND ADJUSTED TO FIT INTO A USABLE AND ACHIEVABLE DAILY AGENDA OF REALISTIC PORTIONS TO COMPLETE. (*AND THE LORD ANSWERED ME, AND SAID, WRITE THE VISION, AND MAKE IT PLAIN UPON TABLES, THAT HE MAY RUN THAT READETH IT*. - HABAKKUK 2:2.)

39. __PAY ATTENTION TO THE SPEED LIMITS:__
KNOW YOUR PACES OF LIFE. IF YOU DO, YOU WILL
NOTICE THAT THERE WILL BE TIMES TO LAUGH
WHILE WALKING AND OTHER TIMES TO BE SERIOUS
WHILE SPRINTING.

40. __KNOWING YOUR IDENTITY IS KEY:__ SEE
YOURSELF NOT NECESSARILY AS YOU ARE NOW,
BUT WHAT YOU WILL BE WHEN YOU ACHIEVE
YOUR DREAM. KNOWING YOUR IDENTITY CAN
TEACH YOU HOW TO ACT TODAY SO THAT YOU
BEGIN TO MATCH HOW YOU SEE YOURSELF IN THE
FUTURE.

41. __STAYING TEACHABLE IS KEY:__ FORCE
YOURSELF TO BE TEACHABLE IN ALL SITUATIONS
DAILY. BY DOING THIS YOU WILL STRETCH
YOURSELF INTO DAILY GROWTH.

42. __WATCH YOUR MOUTH:__ THE WISE IN HEART
WILL TEACH THEMSELVES TO SPEAK CORRECT
WORDS. THEY WILL EXPAND THEMSELVES WITH
SOUND KNOWLEDGE.

43. __ATTENTION SINGLES:__ THE NUMBER ONE
CAUSE THAT I HAVE SEEN THAT LEADS PEOPLE
INTO THE WRONG RELATIONSHIP OR A BAD
RELATIONSHIP IS THE LACK OF __PATIENCE.__

44. IF YOU STRIVE TO OBTAIN WISDOM AS
THOUGH IT IS A BURIED TREASURE; YOU WILL HAVE
GOOD SUCCESS IN YOUR LIFE.

45. THE SECRET TO *GOOD SUCCESS* IS NOT BY HOLDING KNOWLEDGE IN YOUR HEAD. BUT RATHER, BY APPLYING KNOWLEDGE THROUGH YOUR ACTIONS.

46. <u>**DON'T LET YOUR EMOTIONS STOP YOU:**</u> DO NOT LET YOUR EMOTIONS CONSTANTLY CONTROL YOUR ACTIONS. INSTEAD, USE YOUR ACTIONS TO CONTROL YOUR EMOTIONS.

47. <u>**SUCCESS IS NOT LUCK:**</u> IT IS A DECISION. THIS STATEMENT IS CONTRARY TO POPULAR BELIEF AND IS USUALLY USED BY THOSE WHO FIND IT EASIER TO SAY THAT SOMEONE BECAME SUCCESSFUL BY LUCK. WHICH IN RETURN IS OFTEN JUST AN EASY EXCUSE TO JUSTIFY ONESELF OF ALL THE REASONS WHY THEY MAY NOT HAVE SUCCEEDED THEMSELVES. "IF I WHERE ONLY LUCKY, I WOULD BE SUCCESSFUL TOO." **NONSENSE, PREPARE YOUR PLAN AND PUT IT IN ACTION!**

48. <u>**YOU CAN COLOR WITH WHATEVER COLORS YOU WANT:**</u> AGAIN, YOU **CAN** CREATE YOUR LIFE TO MATCH WHAT YOU WANT. SO WHY NOT PURPOSE IN YOUR HEART TO CREATE YOUR LIFE, RELATIONSHIPS, BUSINESS, OR ENDEAVORS TO BE FUN, REWARDING, AND EXACTLY WHAT YOU WANT?

49. <u>**UNLIMITED SOURCE:**</u> GOD IS AS MUCH AS YOU NEED HIM TO BE, AND FOR THIS REASON, DO NOT BE AFRAID OF HAVING DREAMS THAT ARE BIGGER THAN YOU.

50. SOME GIFTS ARE GIVEN AND SOME EARNED:
IF YOU WANT TO WIN IN LIFE YOU MUST REALIZE
THAT THERE ARE EARNED GIFTS THAT GOD GIVES
US. WE OFTEN GET DESIRES IN OUR HEART THAT
SIMPLY MUST BE DEVELOPED, EVEN IF IT FORCES
US OUT OF OUR COMFORT ZONE.

51. NO DREAM IS TOO BIG UNLESS YOUR BELIEF
AND DESIRE ARE TOO SMALL. — *DUSTIN LEE*

52. UNLESS YOU CONSISTENTLY TRY SOMETHING
NEW, YOU WON'T GROW. CONTINUE TO STRETCH
YOURSELF EVEN IF IT HURTS. AND REMEMBER
THIS, ONCE A RUBBER BAND IS STRETCHED IT WILL
NEVER RETURN TO IT'S ORIGINAL SIZE.

53. THIS IS HOW ACHIEVERS GET WAY AHEAD:
MAKE IT A HABIT TO MAKE THE MOST OF THE DAY,
EVERYDAY.

54. "I CAN'T CHANGE" IS JUST A POOR EXCUSE FOR
NOT SUCCEEDING. I'M HERE TO TELL YOU, YES YOU
CAN! NOT ONLY CAN YOU CHANGE, YOU CAN HAVE
GOOD SUCCESS AND IT WILL BE WORTH IT!

55. IF YOU DREAM WITH HUNGER AND DESIRE FOR
ACTION, THE REALITY WILL BE YOURS.

56. BE FAITHFUL WHERE YOU'RE AT: IF YOU
SAY THAT YOU WANT SUCCESS AND ARE CUR-
RENTLY WORKING FOR SOMEONE ELSE, WHY NOT
PERFECT YOUR WORK ETHICS WHILE YOU ARE
THERE? WORK HARD FOR THAT PERSON FOR THESE
REASONS: THE WAY YOU PERFORM NOW BECOMES

HABIT FORMING AND WILL BECOME THE WAY YOU PERFORM LATER. LAZY PERFORMANCE PRODUCES LAZINESS AND DILIGENT PERFORMANCE PRODUCES DILIGENCE.

57. A WISE PERSON WILL LISTEN, HEAR, AND INCREASE KNOWLEDGE. A WISE PERSON WITH UNDERSTANDING WILL CONTINUALLY SEEK WISE COUNSEL.

58. A SUPER-ACHIEVER IS A PERSON WHO KEEPS WORKING IN SPITE OF DIFFICULTIES AND DISTRACTIONS. — *PASTOR TOMMY BARNETT*.

59. A GREAT CAUSE DOES NOT DRIVE YOU, IT DRAWS YOU.
— *PASTOR TOMMY BARNETT*.

60. IT'S NOT THE POSITION WHO MAKES THE MAN, IT'S THE MAN WHO MAKES THE POSITION.
— *PASTOR TOMMY BARNETT*

61. THOSE WHO COME UP WITH AN EXCUSE ARE DEFEATED BEFORE THEY EVER GET STARTED.

62. FIRST WE MUST BE HONEST WITH OURSELVES, THEN WE CAN ALWAYS BE HONEST WITH OTHERS.

63. BEFORE CHANGES CAN EFFECTIVELY BE MADE IN ANY AREA OF LIFE, WE MUST FIRST DECIDE TO BE BRUTALLY HONEST WITH OURSELVES. IT STARTS BY IDENTIFYING AND EXPOSING WHO WE ARE, AGAINST WHO WE SHOULD BE. SO OFTEN IN THIS AREA WE CAN LIE TO OURSELVES AND LIVE

LIFE AS A FAIRYTALE BY PRETENDING THAT WE
DON'T HAVE ISSUES. EVERYBODY HAS ISSUES TO
SOME EXTENT, FOR SOME IT MAY BE THE HABIT OF
BLAMING THE WORLD FOR THEIR PROBLEMS OR
LIVING A DRAMA THAT THEIR ALWAYS A VICTIM
OF OTHERS DOINGS. OFTEN TIMES IT'S JUST A
HABIT OR FORM OF MANIPULATION TO MAKE
PEOPLE FEEL SORRY FOR THEM, AND IN MANY
CASES IT'S THAT INDIVIDUALS WAY OF AVOIDING
THE FACT THAT THEY MAY BE THE ONE WITH A
PROBLEM. IF YOU HAVE ANY PROBLEMS, WHY NOT
JUST EXPOSE THEM AND MAKE CHANGES, THEN
YOU CAN LIVE EFFECTIVELY?

64. BE CAREFUL OF THE THINGS, SITUATIONS, OR
HABITS IN LIFE THAT MAY ROB YOU OF CLARITY.

65. REMEMBER, WE ALL HAVE THE POTENTIAL TO
SUCCEED AT SOMETHING IN LIFE. THERE WILL
NEVER BE ANOTHER YOU; GOD HAS PLACED
SOMETHING DEEP WITHIN ALL OF US THAT MAKES
US UNIQUE AND VALUABLE.

66. BELIEF AND ATTITUDE IS EVERYTHING.
BELIEF IS YOUR POWER OF CERTAINTY AND
ATTITUDE IS YOUR RESPONSE FROM CERTAINTY.

67. IF YOU'RE HAVING TROUBLE SUCCEEDING IN
YOUR OWN LIFE GOALS, WHY NOT HELP SOMEONE
ELSE REACH THEIRS, ONE WHO WILL HELP YOU
ACHIEVE YOURS IN THE PROCESS?

68. SUCCESS AND FAILURE ARE A PART OF LIFE
AND FAILING CAN BE A HUMBLING EXPERIENCE.
SOMETIMES ALL WE CAN DO IS TAKE THE TIME TO

LEARN FROM THE FAILURES AND BE SURE TO
NEVER LET THEM HAPPEN AGAIN.

69. THE MORE ORGANIZED YOU ARE, THE MORE
PRODUCTIVE YOU WILL BECOME. GOOD
PRODUCTIVITY CAN ONLY LEAD TO PROSPERITY
AND THE ATTAINMENT OF *GOOD SUCCESS*.

70. IN ORDER TO STAY ON SCHEDULE, ALL YOU
HAVE TO DO ON A DAILY BASIS IS MAKE SURE
THAT YOU ARE ACCOMPLISHING THE RIGHT
AMOUNT OF WORK AND DOING IT ON THE BEST
AND MOST APPROPRIATE PATH.

71. TRUE INTEGRITY IS WHO YOU ARE WHEN NO
ONE IS LOOKING.

72. **CHANGE DOESN'T STOP AT A DIPLOMA:** LIFE
INVOLVES CONSTANT CHANGE. IF WE DO NOT
CONTINUE TO MOVE UPWARD WE WILL FIND
OURSELVES LEFT BEHIND.

73. **PIONEER YOUR TRAILS TO FREEDOM:**
DISCOVER THE CLARITY OF FOLLOWING TRAIL
SIGNS WHICH CAN BE FOUND BY SPENDING PRIME
TIME IN THINKING, IT'S THESE THOUGHTS THAT
WILL EXPLAIN SOUND LOGIC FOR YOU TO BASE
YOUR DECISIONS ON. BY DOING THIS, YOU WILL
ALWAYS BE GOING IN THE RIGHT DIRECTION.

74. **ENJOY THE MOMENT:** YOU CAN ACHIEVE
YOUR POTENTIAL BY FOCUSING ON THE FUTURE
BUT ALSO LIVING FOR TODAY.

75. ALWAYS REPLACE A NEGATIVE WITH A POSITIVE AND NEVER ALLOW YOURSELF TO BELIEVE THAT THERE IS NO SOLUTION TO YOUR PROBLEMS.

76. **FREEDOM OF YOUR TIME HAS A PRICE:** IF YOU WANT MORE TIME OFF THAN JUST WEEKENDS, I SUGGEST YOU SERIOUSLY CONSIDER LEARNING HOW TO EARN THE WAGES OF WEEKS AND MONTHS IN DAYS. IT **CAN** AND **IS** BEING DONE BY MANY WHO HAVE MASTERED THE ART OF DUPLICATING THEIR TIME AND EFFORTS AND SO CAN YOU!

77. THERE **ARE** MORE MONEY TRAILS FOR PICKING UP EXTRA MONEY TODAY THAN **EVER**. WHICH TRAIL WILL YOU PICK? PENNY TRAILS, QUARTER TRAILS, DOLLAR TRAILS, 100 DOLLAR TRAILS, 1,000 DOLLAR TRAILS, OR MORE?

78. **BE THANKFUL, NOT GREEDY:** IN GIVING OR RECEIVING WE MUST REMEMBER THAT THE THOUGHT & INTENSIONS ARE MORE IMPORTANT THAN THE ACTUAL GIFT. NEVER BECOME SO GREEDY THAT YOU OVER LOOK A PERSONS HEART.

79. **GOODS AND BADS OF MATERIALISM:** IN ATTAINING POSSESSIONS, IT'S OK IF THE THINGS YOU GET ARE USED TO ENJOY LIFE AND LOVE PEOPLE. IT'S NOT OK IF YOU LOSE YOUR CONCERN FOR PEOPLE AND START USING PEOPLE JUST SO THAT YOU CAN LOVE THINGS.

80. GOD REACHES OUT: HANG ONTO THE HANDS OF GOD BECAUSE HE'S TRYING TO HANG ONTO YOU. HE NEVER GIVES UP ON US, BUT OFTEN, IT'S

US THAT GIVES UP ON HIM, ESPECIALLY WHEN HE'S TRYING TO TEACH US SOMETHING THAT WE NEED TO LEARN IN ORDER TO MAINTAIN GOOD SUCCESS THROUGHOUT LIFE.

81. THE IMPORTANCE OF LISTENING IS OBVIOUS. WE HAVE TWO EARS AND ONE MOUTH.

82. REMEMBER THE STORY OF DAVID AND GOLIATH? THE MAJORITY THOUGHT GOLIATH WAS TOO BIG, BUT DAVID THOUGHT HE WAS TOO BIG TO MISS.

83. DEVELOPING RESPONSIBILITY IS ONE OF THE MAIN INGREDIENTS IN THE RECIPE FOR *GOOD SUCCESS*, AND IT CAN BE LEARNED BY EVERYONE.

84. COMPLETING YOUR DAILY TASKS IS CRUCIAL IN REGARDS TO REACHING SUCCESS. YOU CAN ALWAYS MAKE MORE MONEY, BUT YOU CAN'T MAKE MORE TIME. THEREFORE TREAT IT WITH RESPECT AND USE IT WISELY.

85. **GO TO THE TOP FOR SUGGESTIONS:** IF YOU WANT THE BEST, WE MUST HAVE A MASTER PLAN OF ACTION. AND IN THIS I STRONGLY SUGGEST YOU OPEN YOUR MIND TO GOD'S SUGGESTIONS FOR YOUR LIFE.

86. **LIFE CAN BE LIKE A VIDEO GAME:** I HAVE ALWAYS FOUND UNEXPECTED ENERGY BY OPERATING MY LIFE IN THIS FASHION. PLAYING THE GAME FORCES YOU TO BE SERIOUS ABOUT OUTSMARTING OBSTACLES AND CRAZY

SITUATIONS. I'M ALSO CONTINUALLY TRYING TO
BREAK MY PERSONAL BEST HIGH SCORES.

87. TALKS CHEAP, IF YOU REALLY WANT TO MAKE
IT IN LIFE YOU MUST LEARN TO BE COMPLETELY
HONEST WITH YOURSELF. IF YOU CAN'T, YOU WILL
ALWAYS BE IN CHAOS AND DISCOMFORT. YOU
CAN'T DEAL WITH WHAT YOU ARE NOT WILLING TO
EXPOSE. MANY HAVE KNOWN THEIR MISSION IN
LIFE BUT DID NOT REACH IT BECAUSE THEY SIMPLY
NEVER TOOK BEING HONEST WITH THEMSELVES
SERIOUSLY.

88. IF YOU REALLY WANT TO WIN YOU MUST BE
SERIOUS ENOUGH TO PUSH YOURSELF INTO DOING
THE MOST PRODUCTIVE ACTIONS AS OFTEN AS
POSSIBLE. CONTINUALLY ASK YOURSELF; WHAT
CAN I DO RIGHT NOW THAT WILL GET ME CLOSER
TO MY GOALS?

89. **DON'T TAKE THINGS FOR GRANTED:** YOU
CAN ALWAYS MAINTAIN YOUR CONFIDENCE BY
CONTINUOUSLY REMINDING YOURSELF THAT YOU
HAVE BEEN UNIQUELY BLESSED WITH BEING THE
CARRIER OF BIG DREAMS. THEN ASK YOURSELF ON
A REGULAR BASIS, WHAT AM I DOING ABOUT
THEM? REMEMBER, TALKS CHEAP!

90. **WE ONLY GET ONE CHANCE:** TO BE
EFFECTIVE WE MUST REALIZE THAT WE ONLY GET
ONE CHANCE TO ACT OUT OUR PREDESTINED PLAN.
OUR LIVES ARE NOT PRACTICE SESSIONS, THEY ARE
THE MAIN EVENT.

91. **MENTAL VACATIONS:** IF YOU EVER FIND YOURSELF BECOMING WEARY, JUST THINK OF THE REWARDS! THERE'S FRIENDS TO ENJOY, VACATIONS TO TAKE, BEACHES TO WALK, HOT AIR BALLOONS TO RISE IN, OCEANS TO SCUBA DIVE, MOUNTAINS TO SKI, LIVES TO SEE IMPROVED — WHATEVER YOUR PLEASURE. THERE'S CONTINUAL JOY AND ENERGY TO DO WHATEVER YOU PUT YOUR MIND TO.

92. **IF THE MIND HAS TRASH TAKE IT OUT:** ALWAYS TAKE THE TIME TO CLEAN OUT THE DEBRIS IN YOUR MIND ON A DAILY BASIS. DO NOT ALLOW PROBLEMS OR WORRIES TO PILE UP WITHOUT BEING DEALT WITH. AGAIN THERE'S ALWAYS SOLUTIONS, FIND THEM AND MOVE ON!

93. CONSTANTLY REMIND YOURSELF THAT YOU'RE WILLING TO DO WHATEVER IT TAKES TO BUILD YOUR DREAMS TO COMPLETION, AND PROVE IT BY YOUR ACTIONS.

94. **REMEMBER WHERE THE HAZARDS ARE:** KNOW THE AREAS OF YOUR LIFE WHERE YOU NEED TO BE STRONGER OR SHARPER. ALSO BE AWARE OF THE PATTERNS OR HABITS OF YOUR LIFE THAT YOU MAY HAVE TROUBLE WITH OR STUMBLE. IF YOU KNOW WHERE YOUR WEAKNESSES ARE, YOU CAN THEN PREPARE YOURSELF TO BE MORE ALERT TO RECOGNIZE THEM WHEN THEY TRY TO RISE UP AGAINST YOU. IF YOU CAN SPOT THEM YOU CAN ALSO OVERCOME THEM.

95. **IT'S ANOTHER MINDSET:** IF YOU ARE LIKE AN EAGLE YOU WILL HAVE TO CATCH A FISH EVERY TIME YOU GET HUNGRY. FAILING TO CATCH A FISH IS DEATH. THIS IS JUST A SAYING BUT TO CONSIDER IT'S REALITY WITHIN OUR OWN LIVES, CAN BECOME THE MAJOR DIFFERENCE BETWEEN JUST WISHING THINGS TO HAPPEN, VERSUS NEEDING THINGS TO HAPPEN. WHEN THINGS BECOME NEEDED THEY HAVE AN AMAZING WAY OF BEING ACCOMPLISHED.

96. **YOU ARE WHAT YOU THINK:** THROUGHOUT THE DAY YOU WILL BECOME EXACTLY WHAT YOU'RE THINKING. MONITOR YOUR THOUGHTS SO YOU CAN DRIVE OUT ALL THE ONES THAT AREN'T POSITIVE OR GEARED TOWARD GOOD SUCCESS.

97. **WHY NOT CONSIDER THE ADDICTION OF GIVING?** GIVERS ARE THE HAPPIEST AND MOST BLESSED PEOPLE. IF YOU LEARN TO GET A BOOST OUT OF GIVING TO HELP OTHERS, YOU WILL FIND THE ENERGY TO ACHIEVE MORE ALONG WITH INCREASED EXCITEMENT BY LIVING VICARIOUSLY THROUGH OTHERS EXCITEMENT.

98. OTHERS CAN'T BENEFIT FROM YOUR EFFORTS IF YOU DON'T SINCERELY STRIVE TO FINISH EVERY DAYS TASKS.

99. **MAKE IMPROVEMENTS WHEN YOU SEE THEM:** KEEP MENTAL PICTURES OF YOUR VISIONS IN THEIR COMPLETED STAGES AND SEE YOURSELF GROWING IN THEM EACH STEP OF THE WAY, LOOK AT THEM OFTEN AND CONTINUOUSLY TAKE NOTES WHEN IMPROVEMENTS ARE DISCOVERED.

100. __EACH DAY__ AS YOU WAKE UP **BE PREPARED** TO MAKE A NEW DECISION. WITHIN THE FIRST FIFTEEN SECONDS OF OPENING YOUR EYES MENTALLY DECIDE THAT YOU ARE WILLING TO STEP INTO THE NEW SELF OF TODAY AND LEAVE THE OLD SELF BEHIND. THANK GOD FOR WHO HE IS AND ALL HE HAS ENTRUSTED YOU WITH. CONSIDER ALL THE THINGS TO BE THANKFUL FOR AND CONSIDER WHAT MUST BE DONE TO MAKE THE MOST OF YOUR DAY, THEN DO IT!

101. OCCASIONALLY WE ARE ALL VISITED BY FEARS & DOUBTS OF THE FUTURE. BUT THIS DOESN'T MEAN WE HAVE TO EXCEPT THEM BECAUSE AT THESE TIMES THAT'S WHERE FAITH & COURAGE CAN COME IN BY OUR CHOICES.

102. THE MINORS OF LIFE ARE IMPORTANT, BUT __NEVER__ ALLOW THE MINORS TO KEEP YOU FROM DOING THE MAJORS.

103. __IMPORTANT KEY:__ FREQUENTLY SCHEDULE IN TIME FOR REFLECTING AND DREAMING, AND DOCUMENT EVERYTHING SO THAT IT IS USABLE BY YOURSELF AS WELL AS THOSE WHO WILL BE YOUR TEAMMATES.

104. IT ISN'T SO MUCH THE PROPER SPEECH THAT GETS YOU AHEAD IN LIFE, BUT MORE SO THE PROPER EFFORT. LOTS OF PEOPLE HAVE THE EDUCATION, BUT LACK THE APPLICATION.

105. IF YOU DON'T KNOW WHETHER OR NOT YOUR HEARING THE VOICE OF GOD, ASK YOURSELF, ARE THERE ANY THINGS IN YOUR LIFE THAT MAY BE PREVENTING YOU FROM HEARING? MAKE A LIST, EXAMPLE: WATCHING TO MUCH TV, SOCIAL- IZING 24 HOURS A DAY, ETC. WHAT THINGS WOULD YOU BE WILLING TO CUT BACK ON OR GIVE UP IF YOU KNEW YOU COULD HEAR WITH MORE CLARITY?

106. **SOLVE THE PUZZLE.** OUR LIVES ARE SIMULAR TO THE PROCESS OF A PUZZLE. GOD HAS THE COMPLETE PICTURE ALREADY IN PLACE AHEAD OF TIME. THROUGH PRAYER, ISOLATION & PONDERING HE SHOWS US THE PIECES ALONG WITH THE ABILITY TO ARRANGE THEM. THE INSIGHTS & KNOWLEDGE OF UNDERSTANDING A PIECE MAY PRESENT ITS SELF AT ANY MOMENT OF THE DAY. PERHAPS IN THE SHOWER, AT LUNCH, THE DRIVE HOME, ON A MOUNTAIN, AND SO ON. IF YOU'RE SERIOUS ABOUT COMPLETING THE PUZZLE, YOU MUST ALWAYS BE READY WITH METHODS OF DOCUMENTATION. CONSIDER USING A TAPE RECORDER, OR ALWAYS HAVING A NOTEBOOK & PENS OR PENCILS AT HAND. IF YOU NEGLECT DOCUMENTATION YOU WILL BE SETTLING FOR A LIFE PUZZLE WITH MISSING PIECES.

107. **KEEP EVERYTHING NEW:** SOMETIMES THINGS DON'T SEEM AS EXCITING WHEN THEY BECOME REAL. WE TEND TO GET USED TO THEM AND TAKE THEM FOR GRANTED. DO NOT FORGET WHERE YOU'VE COME FROM AND WHAT IT TOOK YOU TO GET THERE. THE SAME GOES FOR RELATIONSHIPS, NEVER FORGET THE CAPTIVATED FEELINGS YOU FELT WHEN YOU FIRST MET YOUR PARTNER.

108. SUCCESSFUL PEOPLE DO THE BEST WITH WHAT THEY'VE GOT, EDUCATED OR NOT. ONE THING THAT I HAVE SEEN TIME AND TIME AGAIN IS THAT ACTION HAS AN AMAZING WAY OF TEACHING US IN THE AREAS WE MAY LACK.

109. SUCCESS REQUIRES DIRECTION, AND AS LONG AS YOU HAVE A MAP YOU CAN GO AS FAR AS YOU ARE WILLING TO TRAVEL.

110. REACHING ***GOOD SUCCESS*** REQUIRES PATIENCE AND DETERMINATION. NO MATTER HOW LONG IT TAKES OR WHATEVER IT TAKES, REMEMBER THIS, IT REALLY IS WORTH IT AND YOU REALLY CAN HAVE WHATEVER YOU WANT OUT OF LIFE. JUST BELIEVE AND CONTINUE TO REACH UP FOR THAT NEXT STEP OF THE LADDER. ALONG THE WAY, I HOPE TO MEET YOU AT THE TOP.

May God be with you in all you do and may your life be expanded until you reach your <u>destiny.</u>

Your friend & advocate,

Bryan Gauthier

Thoughts & Notes

IF YOU CONTINUE TO DO THE SAME THINGS AND
EXPECT BETTER RESULTS, IT WILL NEVER HAPPEN.
BEFORE WE CAN MOVE FORWARD WITH SUCCESS
HABITS, WE MUST FIRST UNLEARN OUR FAILURE
HABITS. I'VE FOUND THE ONLY EFFECTIVE WAY TO
BREAK A HABIT IS TO REPLACE IT
WITH ANOTHER HABIT.

HTTP://WWW.BETTERPATHS.COM

Thoughts & Notes

UNDERSTAND THAT THROUGH LIFE YOU HAVE TO
CONSTANTLY REFOCUS YOURSELF IN THE DIRECTION
YOU WANT TO GO. BEWARE OF BECOMING
SIDETRACKED.

Thoughts & Notes

DON'T SWEAT PETTY CRITICISM. "IF CRITICISM HAD
ANY REAL POWER, THE SKUNK WOULD HAVE BEEN
EXTINCT YEARS AGO."
— MARK TWAIN

*"HAPPY IS THE MAN THAT FINDETH WISDOM,
AND THE MAN THAT GETTETH UNDERSTANDING.
FOR THE MERCHANDISE OF IT IS BETTER THAN
THE MERCHANDISE OF SILVER, AND THE GAIN
THEREOF THAN FINE GOLD.
SHE IS MORE PRECIOUS THAN RUBIES:
AND ALL THE THINGS THOU CANST DESIRE ARE
NOT TO BE COMPARED UNTO HER.
LENGTH OF DAYS IS IN HER RIGHT HAND;
AND IN HER LEFT HAND RICHES AND HONOUR.
HER WAYS ARE WAYS OF PLEASANTNESS,
AND ALL HER PATHS ARE PEACE."*

THOUGHTS & NOTES

THOUGHTS & NOTES

Section 4

12 Personalized Teachings For Good Success

By

Bryan J. Gauthier

12 Personalized Teachings For
Good Success

NUMBER ONE: ATTITUDE

Can you keep a good attitude even when things get rough? If your answer is no, be aware of this, attitude is at least 90% of what makes people successful or unsuccessful. If your attitude cannot be controlled, your chances of reaching good success will also be out of control and far from your grasp. The main ingredient for what makes people successful is found between our two ears, in our thinking. I've watched many people, including myself go through hardships and challenges that would make a lot of people act as though they have been shot in the chest and left with no hope. Yet they still continue to press on and rise above the challenges. Why? Because of attitude, your attitude will either pull you down or pull you through, the most challenging situations in life. In most cases people give up on life because they let their attitude get the best of them. Attitude can be a choice, it may not always be easy, but it can be developed until it becomes easier unto the point of habit. The next time you want to get mad, sad or flustered about something, ask yourself if by doing so, will it make things any better or get you any closer to where you want to go? Do you know that having a bad attitude takes a lot of energy? This same energy can be used for achieving toward a purpose & getting yourself closer to personal success. One of the biggest energy robbers I know of is traffic, actually it's not the traffic, but more so the attitudes of people who allow the traffic to take control of their minds. When I'm in traffic I will do what I can do, but after that I will accept the fact that getting mad is not going to make anything any better. I've made it a habit to use the same time and energy it takes to get mad or stressed out, to listen to a teaching tape or enjoy the scenery of the city or the skyline. Q: Why not challenge yourself from this day to develop an addiction to keeping a better attitude in all the situations you're confronted with? If we can learn to smile through the things we normally don't feel like smiling through, we will soon find ourselves smiling all the time, instinctively by realizing that things really aren't all that bad and they could be worse.

Fill in the blanks as follows: List every area you can think of where you have slipped up regarding a good attitude. After you finish go back and ponder over each one, keep in mind that any negative thinking patterns can be like poison to your plans and they should be corrected. In column A write down any areas in which you struggle with maintaining a positive attitude. In column B write down how you can improve your attitude, or by changing how you think about that particular situation.

A. Example:
I get frustrated easily
in traffic

B: Solution:
Listen to a teaching tape

1. _____

2. _____

3. _____

4. _____

5. _____

6. _____

7. _____

8. _____

1. _____

2. _____

3. _____

4. _____

5. _____

6. _____

7. _____

8. _____

Thoughts & Notes

Number Two: Put It Into Action

Are you a person who talks your way out of your own ideas? People often talk about what they are going to do, and most of the time to the wrong people. If you share a good idea with someone who is an achiever, most likely they will say that's a great idea and give advice on how to make it happen. But on the other hand, if you share it with negative people or unhappy people, the responses you get will normally be based on who they are and what they think. Sometimes all it takes is one negative comment to destroy a good idea or damage our enthusiasm. So often we look for a starting point or the approval of those around us to decide whether or not we will do anything with a good idea. A strong point to remember is this, be cautious with the opinion or approval from someone who is less successful or has less experience than you. Be cautious of depending on the approval from those who aren't going in a similar direction as you. Would you ask a diesel mechanic for their opinion if you needed medical treatment for a rare life threatening disease? Of course not, you would go to someone with knowledge and experience in that particular area. I know it's hard at times to not share exciting ideas with those around us, but at times we need to protect the idea until it is set in motion and on its way to completion. In most cases, it's our actions that will have the best means of explaining ourselves to others. Spend more time putting your idea into action and less time into telling, unless you truly know that those you share it with are going to help with advice on making it happen, rather than advice for not making it happen. There's a time for thinking and planning and there's also a time for action. List your ideas in the blanks that follow, and then list your plans of action.

A. List your ideas:

1. _____
2. _____
3. _____
4. _____
5. _____
6. _____
7. _____
8. _____

B. List the first steps for getting started

1. _____
2. _____
3. _____
4. _____
5. _____
6. _____
7. _____
8. _____

Thoughts & Notes

Number Three:
Make Your Life A Real Game, You Must Win

Why not make your life like a game, titled "I Will Win." The attitude in which we look at things can make all the difference in the world. Instead of just going through the motions, I have changed my outlook on task to be like a game, one that I take very seriously, yet have fun. Learn to like the maneuvers and your abilities involved to complete each day's task and responsibilities, look at them as though you are trying to break a high score that you may have set the last time you played. Everyday, the more you become familiar with today's course and it's obstacles, you will start to instinctively be able to handle more and more responsibilities. You will do so by the ability to enjoy them as thrills because you have changed your whole outlook to be as a conscious experience of the "I Will Win" game. All aspects of the real life game become personally challenging and competitive toward improving your score. Getting your mail, or doing your chores as quickly as possible suddenly becomes a fun obsession and habits focused on beating the time it took you before. Finishing daily tasks in the order of their importance suddenly becomes a routine that gets easier and easier as you find yourself getting better and more equipped.

Q: What can I do in my life to add more productive points to my quest for breaking my "Personal Best Records"? (List some areas you can begin working on today.)

A:

1. _____
2. _____
3. _____
4. _____
5. _____
6. _____
7. _____
8. _____

Thoughts & Notes

NUMBER FOUR: SET A GUARD TO STAND WATCH AT THE GATES TO YOUR MIND

Don't allow other people to bring you down from God-likeness when you are trying to create something from nothing through your imagination. Avoid letting unproductive thoughts and mindless activities occupy your time. Don't listen to any negative input that is counter-productive to what you are striving to obtain. Learn to identify those things that may hinder or slow down your progress toward your dreams and goals. Identify the negative and then send it on its way "access denied." There will always be the times of having people in our lives that are chronically critical by nature. These people, by habit spew garbage out of their mouths faster than they can think. Be cautious of negative or bad influences, because letting garbage into the fertile soil of your mind may cause your plans to become deteriorated or filled with confusion. For this reason alone we all need a quality control department working full time in the facility of our minds. Every time you are faced with or confronted by small, negative, and doubtful thinking be aware that your goals are in jeopardy of being undermined and attacked. Sometimes we can correct the negativity in those around us by simply confronting them on how you feel toward their attitude and remarks. Then other times we can talk until we are blue in the face. If that's the case, don't waste your time, keep good character and move on. Get your thoughts refocused back on your mission at hand. The bigger and more important your dream is to you, will determine how strong your mind is in removing negative input immediately, rather than entertaining it and risking it's effects. By staying focused you will wake up with more enthusiasm and have more energy because your dream will draw you toward your destiny. Your dream alone will produce energy in your body even greater than food can achieve.

Q: Am I willing to build up in the required mental reserves to commit whatever it takes to stay Positive and Teachable?

A: Yes _____ No _____

Q: Do I truly let people's comments influence my decisions and commitments toward going all out like I was designed to do?

A: Yes _____ Sometimes _____ No _____

Q: What can I do or think of that would keep my mind more disciplined or under control?

A:_____

_____

_____

_____

_____

_____

_____

_____

_____

_____

_____

_____

_____

_____

_____

_____

_____

_____

_____

_____

_____

_____

_____

Thoughts & Notes

NUMBER FIVE: THINK BEYOND THE JOB MENTALITY

For some of us all we have ever known growing up is, what we should do to get a job. It's very rare to have heard anyone ask, have you ever considered starting your own business? Throughout our school years most of our education was geared toward getting a good job. If you want to get a good job, you have to learn this or if you want to get hired by a good company you have to know this. When most of us think of a job, we tend to think of making so much per hour, working eight hours a day, five days a week. Thinking like this makes it hard to comprehend what free enterprise is, because it's totally different. Free enterprise is night and day from the traditional nine to five job mentality. In free enterprise you have no limits, you can go as far as your willing to travel. The traditional working by the hour for a certain wage now becomes working by the concept. The concept can be making $30,000 every month or every other month by selling a piece of land while working a few hours a day or a few days per month. The concept can be that of marketing a product through the Home Depot warehouses within your state or through all 900 plus worldwide. The concept can be that of having a mail order or Internet business that earns five times your current salary just by working each Saturday to fill orders. Do you see my point? The education we attained in school was very important, but most will hang that diploma on the wall and think that they're through. Well their not, that's just the beginning. The studying and working hard part was important for the purpose of getting you in the habit of seeking and finding answers. In free enterprise if you do your homework and how you do your homework, determines how much you get paid. I enjoy doing my homework ten times more now than I did when I was in school! Why? Because it's worth it, it's beyond worth it! Even if you are currently at a job, keep in mind a lot of us started our businesses by working on Saturdays. What started out small soon became full time, actually four-hour days on average.

Q: If I could start a part time business working just Saturdays, how much would I be content with earning for that day?

A: $_____ per day

Q: If I could earn that amount each Saturday while doubling that amount each month, how long would it be before I considered going full time?

A: _____ months

Q: List three business ideas you could see yourself doing on Saturdays.

A: 1. _____   2. _____   3. _____

Q: When could you start by, at the latest?

A: day_____ month_____ year_____

Thoughts & Notes

NUMBER SIX: IF YOU DON'T KNOW, ASK QUESTIONS

Do you have questions about the process of how something can be manufactured? Look in the Yellow Pages or on the Internet under the categories of manufactures closely related to what you're thinking about having done. Call them and ask questions, if they don't know they probably know someone who does. Do you have questions about getting your office set up so that it is organized and usable? Go into any business similar to what you are interested in doing and ask their advice.
Most people achieving things or doing things well, love to share advice. There is an unlimited amount of answers waiting to be heard all around us. Everything we need to know is usually found in or through the people around us everyday. If one person doesn't have the answer to what you need, most likely they will be able to get you closer to what you need, by offering you contacts to find what you're looking for. Make it a habit to ask questions wherever and whenever the opportunity presents itself to learn more about information relating to your mission in life.

Q: Whom do I know that would be the best starting point to find out answers or names of contacts that could provide answers to what I'm trying to figure out?

A: (List the names of contacts and what they might be able to answer.)

Names: **Possible answers:**

1. _____   1. _____
2. _____   2. _____
3. _____   3. _____
4. _____   4. _____
5. _____   5. _____

Thoughts & Notes

Number Seven: Write Things
Down So It's Usable

Those that don't write things down will get passed by those who do. We cripple ourselves by not writing things down. When we write things down, it's almost as if by magic that a piece of paper becomes a video game screen awaiting our strategic adjustments. Whether it's your bills, problems, or thoughts of creating something from nothing, writing it on paper puts things into perspective and suddenly everything seems to be reachable. If you have bills, write them all down and look at them asking, what do I have to do to get rid of them. Problems, write them down along with solution scenarios. "There's a solution to every problem, it just has to be discovered." It is important to write down every idea, even if it's unorganized. Every detail is important because once you get them documented you will be able to expand and improve on them until they become usable. Everything from thoughts to goals can become attainable by taking bite size chunks toward your success based off of what you have written down on paper. If you want to succeed, documentation needs to become a habit. No matter where I go or what I do; I always have a means of documenting my thoughts. The best and most used device I have is a digital voice recorder, which holds at least an hour and a half of recordings. I have made it mandatory to keep this recorder with me wherever I go. Driving, sleeping, at the gym, or running errands, I always have it near me. I can't count how many times I have woken up in the middle of the night or first thing in the morning with valuable pieces of the puzzle, and have simply reached over to press record. In most cases when I wake up again or the day goes by, I don't have a clue what it was that I recorded earlier, and in some cases neither will you. Thoughts do and will, come at the strangest times and places throughout the days. Be prepared to capture them, either by a pencil or recorder. If you use a recorder make sure that you don't allow yourself to record too much without transferring it to paper, or a computer.

Q: How many areas of my life can I think of that could be categorized, needing solutions?

A: Examples: Marketing Plan, Personality Improvements, Morals, etc.

1. _____

2. _____

3. _____

4. _____

5. _____

6. _____

7. _____

8. _____

9. _____

10. _____

11. _____

12. _____

13. _____

14. _____

15. _____

Thoughts & Notes

Task Needing Completion In Order of Importance

1.	11.
2.	12.
3.	13.
4.	14.
5.	15.
6.	16.
7.	17.
8.	18.
9.	19.
10.	20.

NUMBER EIGHT: MAKE THIS DAY COUNT

Make it a habit to strive for getting the most out of every day, day after day. A lot of us have disadvantages in life that force us to outsmart our circumstances. If you are short on time to put toward investing in yourself, learn to multiply your efforts from short time spent to equal more time spent. Be systematic, be consistent and don't go to bed without completing what you personally agreed to do. If you get in bed and there's one thing you still have to get done, go do it. By doing it you can wake up the next day knowing that you can count on yourself to do what you say you will do. Make it a habit to use a daily to do list with an evaluation system. We have provided an example as follows, to use or modify so that it works and is usable for you.

Daily to Do List & Evaluation Form

(Daily to-dos)

1. _____   **"MAKE EVERY DAY WORTHY**
2. _____   **OF YOUR POTENTIAL"**
3. _____   **"COMPLETE TO COMPETE"**
4. _____
6. _____   **(Extra Credit To-Do's)**
7. _____   1._____
8. _____   2._____
9. _____   3._____
10._____   **(New Ideas)**
                      1._____
                      2._____
                      3._____

Daily Scoring: Complete 1-10
All items listed completed = **100%** (**A+**) meaning **A**bove **A**verage.
All items but one completed = **75%** (**C**) meaning **C**ould of done it.
All items but two completed = **50%** (**F**) meaning **F**orgot the importance of the vision.

Extra Credit to-do's: Equal 5 points. These are task that put you ahead of the game.

MAKE THIS DAY COUNT: (CONTINUED)

CAUTION: There can be a down side of making "To-Do Lists". We must learn to stretch ourselves, yet be realistic. If you find yourself at the end of the day with several items left undone or several hours of work needing to be done. Re-evaluate your list, ask yourself why items were left undone. Was it because you got distracted throughout the day, was it laziness or did the work just take longer than you expected? Don't let your list overwhelm you. Sometimes starting a little smaller allows us the time to gauge our efforts and build our confidence with small successes.

Q: What do I need to get done within the next month?

Write down the things you know have to be done to get you closer to your goal, then break them down into bite size chunks, to be completed within your days.

_____

_____

_____

_____

_____

_____

_____

_____

Thoughts & Notes

Task Needing Completion In Order of Importance

1.		11.	
2.		12.	
3.		13.	
4.		14.	
5.		15.	
6.		16.	
7.		17.	
8.		18.	
9.		19.	
10.		20.	

NUMBER NINE: NO NEGATIVE FRIENDS IN YOUR DAILY ROUTINE

If you interact with a lot of people each day your chances of running into some that are negative are almost certain. That's life and we can't let them bring us down. People can change, especially if you can stay positive on a regular basis and those that may be negative see it. Eventually it will rub off to some extent, but during the times that your trying to get your head together make it a standard not to have or allow negative friends to be around you on a regular basis. If they can be corrected, then hang in there, but if not get them out of your life until you can fully help yourself. At least long enough to where you can stand firm on what you know and believe in order to handle their negativity long enough to help them snap out of it. In the beginning stages, the only way I have found to get stronger is to be by myself or get myself around those who are doing or have done more than myself. By doing this the only influence you get is positive and mainly interested in finding solutions or ways to make your ideas work. With people like that around, a lot of time is saved because they already know things are possible and instead of wasting your time telling you all the reasons in the world why it won't work. They can spend the same time giving you insights of what might make it easier to get the job done and how to do it faster. Keep in mind, iron sharpens iron.

Q: Do I have close friends that are around me on a daily basis with negative attitudes?

A: Yes_____ No_____

Q: Can I change them or set them straight so that I can be more focused?

A: Yes_____ No_____

Q: Whom do I know or admire that may be willing to mentor, guide, or influence me toward reaching Good Success? **A:**

Thoughts & Notes

Number Ten: Become Addicted To Helping Others

The happiest people I've seen yet are those who love to give or help others. Successful tightwads are never happy regardless of how much they make. When you get into the habit of giving you will soon learn that it becomes addicting, and it will motivate you to make more money. Almost any form of giving excites most successful people, whether it's giving out counsel to someone who is teachable or simply leaving a $100.00 tip to someone you believe in. The secret to being motivated all the time is closely related to giving to others. When we give to those who use it properly, we tend to find ourselves living vicariously through their excitement, which in return gives us more excitement. Knowing that the more we make in life will improve the lives of those around us we can't help but to have that extra incentive to work harder. People can still become wealthy in life with an all about themselves attitude, but they are missing out on an incredible ingredient. That ingredient provides tremendous amounts of extra energy and personal satisfaction that can only be attained through achieving for others as well as ourselves. There are also many proven life principles about giving to people taught in the bible, whatever you give out will always come back increased. I am 100% convinced that I am successful not because of how hard I work, although that is important, the main reason, I believe, is because I have established giving programs in my life that are mandatory. Giving is the most secure form of investing I have seen yet. I have seen a lot of people work pretty much as hard as me yet not advance, I believe this is because of their motives of why they want money. If you want to see if someone or yourself has that special extra driving force to succeed financially, ask why do you want to be rich? The ones who stay energized on a long-term basis can answer as follows, to be able to have a better lifestyle for myself and all those I come in contact with throughout my life.

Q: What forms of giving can you think of, that would fill a need for people around you now, and possibly in communities later?

A: Fill a need for people around you. (Example: Buy a certain family $200.00 worth of groceries.)

1._____
2._____
3._____
4._____
5._____
6._____
7._____
8._____

A: Fill a need for communities later. (Example: Sponsor an inner city outreach program.)

1._____
2._____
3._____
4._____
5._____
6._____
7._____
8._____

Thoughts & Notes

NUMBER ELEVEN:
MONEY IS WORTHLESS
WITHOUT YOUR HEALTH

We must all have a balance in every area of our life when striving for success; it's the balance that changes success to good success. You can have all the money in the world, but without your health it is pretty much worthless. I have met people who became very successful in their business, yet their quality of life is awful because of how poorly they treated their bodies during the pursuit. Until you become established, success may demand that you work long hours for days and weeks at a time more or less, depending on how much you want. Regardless of what it may take in your life, be wise enough to set aside time to exercise and eat properly. It is very easy to get into a rut of eating garbage foods and not exercising, only to realize one day that your body does not feel even close to healthy, but rather old and burned out. Make it a priority, health first, because without your health success is no fun and pretty much worthless.

Q: What is my ideal body weight in which I know is healthy?

A: _____ pounds

Q: What means of diet and exercise do I plan to use to maintain that weight throughout my life?

A:_____

_____

_____

For additional study in becoming "**A Healthier You**"…read our study course:
> "*Fastest Muscle Growth & Body Toning Naturally.*"
> ## GREAT HEALTH = GREAT SUCCESS!

To purchase this book, visit our website below.

Thoughts & Notes

NUMBER TWELVE: KNOW YOUR MISSION IN LIFE

Principal number twelve is definitely the most important principle involved for reaching good success. Understanding it requires our total dependency upon God. Did you know that in the bible God tells us that if we want to have good success, we can and it's guaranteed. God also makes it clear that every word he speaks is pure, and it can be found in the book of Proverbs, chapter 30, verse 5. What he's saying is that he does not and cannot lie. According to God's word we can positively have good success guaranteed with one little exception. That exception can also be found in the book of <u>Proverbs, chapter 16, verse 3</u>. Read it for yourself, it says: *"Commit thy works unto the Lord, and thy thoughts shall be established."* Almost all the other insights I have listed are principles straight from the bible, and geared to bring you directly to the understanding of number twelve's universal truth. There are plenty of man made philosophies in the world today, but the only truths that have continued to stand the test of time and all levels of technology or advancements in civilization is the word of God. In the book of <u>Isaiah, chapter 55, verses 8 & 9</u> God says this: *"For my thoughts are not your thoughts, neither are your ways my ways, saith the Lord. For as the heavens are higher than the earth, so are my ways higher than your ways, and my thoughts than your thoughts."* God is a father and he wants to bless us in every area of our lives, but in order to do that he has to get us to stop living our lives based off of our own understanding. He sees exactly what it takes for us to have good success in every area of our lives. He sees what it will take for us to be at our happiest if we are to be married successfully long term. He sees what it will take if we are to live and be healthy long term. He sees what it will take if we are to be financially stable long term. He knows what we need to do to be the happiest in all areas of our life, and he knows it better than us, his thoughts are without blemish. He also knows how to keep us from hell. God has always given us freedom of choice to live in heaven on earth through our choices or to live in hell on earth through our choices. In the bible he teaches us how to hear his voice for guidance. His word says in Proverbs, chapter 8, verses 1 through 21 this: *"Doth not wisdom cry? And understanding put forth her voice? She standeth on the top of high places, by the way in the places of the paths. She crieth at the gates, at the entry of the city, at the coming in at the doors. Unto you, O men, I call; and my voice is to the sons of man. O ye simple, understand wisdom: and, ye fools, be ye of an understanding heart. Hear; for I will speak of excellent things; and the opening of my lips shall be right things. For my mouth shall speak truth; and wickedness is an abomination to my lips. All the words of my mouth are in righteousness; there is nothing forward or perverse in them. They are all plain to him that understandeth, and right to them that find knowledge. Receive my instruction, and not silver; and knowledge rather than choice gold. For wisdom is better than rubies; and all things that may be desired are not to be compared to it. I wisdom dwell with prudence, and find out knowledge of witty inventions. The fear of the Lord is to hate evil: pride, and arrogancy, and the evil way, and the forward mouth, do I hate. Counsel is mine, and sound wisdom: I am understanding; I have strength. By me kings reign, and princes decree justice. By me princes rule, and nobles, even all the judges of the earth. I love them that love me; and those that seek me early shall find me. Riches and honour are with me; yea, durable riches and righteousness. My fruit is better than gold, yea, than fine gold; and my revenue than choice silver. I lead in the way of righteousness, in the midst of the paths of judgment: That I may cause those that love me to inherit substance; and I will fill their treasures"*. That is just a sliver from God's word. People all around the world spend thousands of dollars on seminars to learn how to make more money or live better lives, when all of it that is true and flawless is right out of the bible. Wisdom is the most important thing we can grab hold of in life and we can start at the beginning by understanding a verse found in Proverbs, chapter 9, verse 10. This verse was given to me by my mentor, Mick Casey who wrote it at the front of a bible he gave me. It took me about twenty times of reading it before it finally clicked and radically changed my ways of living from night to day. It states this: *"The fear of the Lord is the beginning of wisdom: and the knowledge of the holy one is understanding"*.   To give you a head start, think of a father who is looking out for your best interest, but he has rules and consequences set, and if he is pure and flawless, he is unable to lie. That means that no matter how much he loves you, he has to follow through with the consequences if we choose to go that path. Also keep this in mind, once you fully comprehend this meaning; realize that it's just the beginning of wisdom. The more we get to know who God really is, the more we get to grasp little tid bits of his understanding, and it is an eternal process. My intentions of exposing this much truth to you is to bring you back to the full understanding of how real it is when talking about good success being guaranteed in your life. The plan that God has created for us through this short stay on earth is fascinating to try and grasp and a challenge to find the best words to properly describe its depths of majestical wonders and entirety. If I had to narrow it down to one word, I suppose the best word I could use would be, (brilliant). The whole process pivots around the simplicities of God and back to the basics of freedom of choice. God has an incredibly magnificent predestined plan already pre-recorded as if it were on audiocassette waiting on a shelf in heaven in a storage facility specially made for containing every person's destiny on earth. Each and every one of us has God given destiny placed within us that makes us unique. The key to unlocking it is through the desire of wanting to know him and having a relationship with him, followed by the commitment of our plans. *"Commit thy works unto the Lord, and thy thoughts shall be established."* The brilliance of God can be clearly seen in the freedom of choice he has entrusted us with. We can choose a path that can lead us through hell on earth through our choices or have all of his understanding and all of his wisdom and all of his perspectives, thoughts and insights, for the purpose of having good success in our lives in every area of our lives, along with partaking in his plan of bringing good success to others through our lives by simply committing our works unto him. And then as if by magic by doing so we move the hand of God to where he takes our predestined plan off of the shelf and inserts it into a spiritual audio player, then pressing play we are able from thereafter to listen and hear detailed step by step instructions of how and what we are to do to fulfill our destiny. The procedure also has a two-fold benefit; we can only hear the instructions by having a real father and child relationship, which draws us to the place of communication with God through pondering and prayer. One of the biggest and most precious aspects of prayer is that of listening. I believe we can have as much of our destinies instructions that we are willing to go in prayer to listen for. This means that if you have the strength and endurance, you can spend an entire night on a mountaintop, sharing your heart, committing your works to God then listening and documenting any instructions he has for you. Habakkuk 2:2 says: *"And the Lord answered me, and said, Write the vision, and make it plain upon tables, that he may run that readeth it."* Commit your works unto the Lord and your thoughts will be established. Knowing what you have just learned is great gain, but I must challenge you in an area that so many fail. It's assuring to know that if we step out in faith we will receive the instructions for where to go and what to do, but that's not enough. I have seen and met people that know more about God and more about there potential than myself, and these same people I have also seen fail or squander that knowledge. How often have you heard the phrase, "knowledge is power"? Well it's not power, at least not by itself. Applied knowledge is power. A lot of people know a lot of things, but without action it's useless. This is something that I realized early on as I listened to a successful man speaking on a teaching tape stating this; "The secret to success is not in knowing, the secret to success is in doing". This truth became evident in my life early on because based on my education and knowledge, fear tried to tell me all the reasons in the world of why not to try and achieve in certain things. We all come against fear at times, but in most cases fear lost in my life because I always took action in the areas that I could, and in the process I learned the knowledge that I was lacking.

Life Changing Questions & Answers

Q: As you progress in life, will you share your proven insights with others who need help? **A:** _____

Q: If there was a leadership role involving effectively reaching and helping others in the same areas that you had been helped, would you consider doing it? **A:** _____
As a Christian, I am wholeheartedly convinced that we exist for the sole purpose of pleasing God and achieving things in our lives that will serve the purposes of Gods plans here and throughout eternity. And knowing this I also believe that we can and will, have all the desires of our heart through this process. God's word tells us in <u>Mathew chapter 6, verse 33,</u>
"But seek first the kingdom of God, and his righteousness; and all these things shall be added unto you." I believe that Good Success starts by knowing God then seeking his direction and plans for our lives. His word says that we can know him through his son, Jesus Christ. I know him, and the Jesus I know is not just some timid painting of a man on a wall but a courageous man, one of discipline, tenacity and love with an open invitation waiting to share his strengths and council to those who would receive him.

Q: If you knew your future held greatness by making Jesus your mentor, would you listen? **A:** _____
Q: Why? **A:** _____

If you have never received Jesus Christ as your personal friend, mentor, counselor, and Savior, why not do it right now? God's word tells us that to know him and have him in our life is easy, all he asks for is sincerity by making a real commitment from your heart, **simply repeat this simple prayer and mean it from your heart and thou shall be saved**. *"Lord Jesus, I believe that you are the Son of God. I believe that you became a man and died on the cross for my sins. I believe that*

God raised you from the dead and made you the Savior of the world. I confess to you now, that I am a sinner and I'm asking you to forgive me, and cleanse me from all the wrongs I have done. Please help me prepare my steps to become a better me. I accept your forgiveness, and from this day forth I receive you as my Mentor, Lord and Savior. In Jesus name I pray, thank you and Amen."

*"...if thou shalt confess with thy mouth, the Lord Jesus, and shalt believe in thine heart that God hath raised him from the dead, thou shalt be saved. For with the heart man believeth unto righteousness; and with the mouth confession is made unto salvation. **"FOR WHOSOEVER SHALL CALL UPON THE NAME OF THE LORD SHALL BE SAVED."** -Romans 10:9,10,13-*

"If we confess our sins, he is faithful and just to forgive us our sins, and to cleanse us from all unrighteousness."
-1 John 1:9-

Now what do I do?

1. Get a bible- and read it daily, it's your spiritual food that will make you strong and able to withstand the challenges of life.
2. Pray, listen and share your thoughts with God daily, he desires for you to know him and to share your heart with him.
3. Help others and share what God teaches you with others.
4. Fellowship with other believers, go to church or get involved with groups where the bible is taught, in its fullness, not customized.
5. Obey his suggestions for your life, let his love effect the lives of others through your good works done through his guidance.
Congratulations, and keep dreaming, never forgetting that you can do it, and it is worth it! May God bless you, encourage you, and complete you until your destiny is reached.

Your friend & advocate, Bryan Gauthier

Section 5

Topics For Organizing Life Goals

By

Bryan J. Gauthier

Topics For Organizing Life Goals

Category Topics as follows:

To Reach This Goal
(Thoughts & Notes)

Task Needing Completion In Order of Importance

1.	11.
2.	12.
3.	13.
4.	14.
5.	15.
6.	16.
7.	17.
8.	18.
9.	19.
10.	20.

MY MAIN LIFE GOAL
& SUB GOALS LEADING TO IT

To Reach This Goal
(Thoughts & Notes)

Task Needing Completion In Order of Importance

1.	11.
2.	12.
3.	13.
4.	14.
5.	15.
6.	16.
7.	17.
8.	18.
9.	19.
10.	20.

MY PRODUCT/SERVICE IDEAS

To Reach This Goal
(Thoughts & Notes)

Task Needing Completion In Order of Importance

1.	11.
2.	12.
3.	13.
4.	14.
5.	15.
6.	16.
7.	17.
8.	18.
9.	19.
10.	20.

MY MEANS OF CONTRIBUTING TO COMMUNITY/HUMANKIND

To Reach This Goal
(Thoughts & Notes)

Task Needing Completion In Order of Importance

1.	11.
2.	12.
3.	13.
4.	14.
5.	15.
6.	16.
7.	17.
8.	18.
9.	19.
10.	20.

MY MANUFACTURING CONTACTS

To Reach This Goal
(Thoughts & Notes)

Task Needing Completion In Order of Importance

1.	11.
2.	12.
3.	13.
4.	14.
5.	15.
6.	16.
7.	17.
8.	18.
9.	19.
10.	20.

MY CUSTOMER PROSPECT LIST

To Reach This Goal
(Thoughts & Notes)

Task Needing Completion In Order of Importance

1.	11.
2.	12.
3.	13.
4.	14.
5.	15.
6.	16.
7.	17.
8.	18.
9.	19.
10.	20.

MY MARKETING IDEAS

To Reach This Goal
(Thoughts & Notes)

Task Needing Completion In Order of Importance

1.	11.
2.	12.
3.	13.
4.	14.
5.	15.
6.	16.
7.	17.
8.	18.
9.	19.
10.	20.

My Key Business Contacts

To Reach This Goal
(Thoughts & Notes)

Task Needing Completion In Order of Importance

1.	11.
2.	12.
3.	13.
4.	14.
5.	15.
6.	16.
7.	17.
8.	18.
9.	19.
10.	20.

My Business Facility Designs

To Reach This Goal
(Thoughts & Notes)

Task Needing Completion In Order of Importance

1.	11.
2.	12.
3.	13.
4.	14.
5.	15.
6.	16.
7.	17.
8.	18.
9.	19.
10.	20.

MY TEAM/STAFF & DEPARTMENTS/DUTIES

To Reach This Goal
(Thoughts & Notes)

Task Needing Completion In Order of Importance

1.	11.
2.	12.
3.	13.
4.	14.
5.	15.
6.	16.
7.	17.
8.	18.
9.	19.
10.	20.

MY WORK/VACATION SCHEDULE

To Reach This Goal
(Thoughts & Notes)

Task Needing Completion In Order of Importance

1.	11.
2.	12.
3.	13.
4.	14.
5.	15.
6.	16.
7.	17.
8.	18.
9.	19.
10.	20.

MY PERSONAL LIFE GOALS PROGRAM

To Reach This Goal
(Thoughts & Notes)

Task Needing Completion In Order of Importance

1.	11.
2.	12.
3.	13.
4.	14.
5.	15.
6.	16.
7.	17.
8.	18.
9.	19.
10.	20.

MY MEANS OF SPIRITUAL GROWTH/MAINTENANCE

To Reach This Goal
(Thoughts & Notes)

Task Needing Completion In Order of Importance

1.	11.
2.	12.
3.	13.
4.	14.
5.	15.
6.	16.
7.	17.
8.	18.
9.	19.
10.	20.

MY MEANS OF RELATIONSHIP GROWTH/MAINTENANCE

To Reach This Goal
(Thoughts & Notes)

Task Needing Completion In Order of Importance

1.	11.
2.	12.
3.	13.
4.	14.
5.	15.
6.	16.
7.	17.
8.	18.
9.	19.
10.	20.

MY IDEAS FOR FAMILY ACTIVITIES/RECREATION

To Reach This Goal
(Thoughts & Notes)

Task Needing Completion In Order of Importance

1.	11.
2.	12.
3.	13.
4.	14.
5.	15.
6.	16.
7.	17.
8.	18.
9.	19.
10.	20.

My Means of Health Improvements/Maintenance

To Reach This Goal
(Thoughts & Notes)

Task Needing Completion In Order of Importance

1.	11.
2.	12.
3.	13.
4.	14.
5.	15.
6.	16.
7.	17.
8.	18.
9.	19.
10.	20.

MY MEANS OF FINANCIAL IMPROVEMENTS/MAINTENANCE

THOUGHTS & NOTES

THOUGHTS & NOTES

THOUGHTS & NOTES

THOUGHTS & NOTES

THOUGHTS & NOTES

THOUGHTS & NOTES

THOUGHTS & NOTES

THOUGHTS & NOTES

THOUGHTS & NOTES

THOUGHTS & NOTES

THOUGHTS & NOTES

THOUGHTS & NOTES

THOUGHTS & NOTES